Amazing Love

Amazing Love

Theology for Understanding Discipleship, Sexuality and Mission

Edited by Andrew Davison
with
Duncan Dormor
Ruth Harley
Rosie Harper
Elizabeth Phillips
Jeff Phillips
Simon Sarmiento
Jane Shaw
Alan Wilson

DARTON · LONGMAN + TODD

First published in 2016 by
Darton, Longman and Todd Ltd
1 Spencer Court
140 – 142 Wandsworth High Street
London SW18 4JJ

ISBN: 978-0-232-53265-4

A catalogue record for this book is available from the British Library

Phototypeset by Kerrypress Ltd, St Albans
Printed and bound by Bell & Bain, Glasgow.

Contents

Authors' Biographies

Andrew Davison is the Starbridge Lecturer in Theology and Natural Sciences at the University of Cambridge, and fellow in theology at Corpus Christi College. He has studied and taught at the Universities of Oxford and Cambridge. He is the author of several books on mission, ecclesiology, pastoral care, and sacramental theology. Since 2015 he has been the canon philosopher of St Albans Cathedral.

Duncan Dormor has been Dean of Chapel at St John's College, Cambridge since 2002. He lectures in the Cambridge Faculty of Divinity on the sociology and anthropology of religion.

Ruth Harley is Children's and Families' Minister at All Saints Church, High Wycombe in the Oxford Diocese, and Chair of Governors at High Wycombe Church of England School. She also leads children's work for On Fire Mission.

Rosie Harper is a former professional singer who is now Vicar of Great Missenden and Chaplain to the Bishop of Buckingham. She has a higher degree in philosophy and ethics from Heythrop College, London, broadcasts on human rights issues, and has served on General Synod since 2010.

Elizabeth Phillips is Tutor in Theology and Ethics at Westcott House and an Affiliated Lecturer in the Faculty of Divinity, University of Cambridge. She is author of *Political Theology: A Guide for the Perplexed* (Continuum, 2012), and co-editor of *The Cambridge Companion to Christian Political Theology* (CUP, 2015).

Jeff Phillips is Tutor in Philosophy and Theology at Westcott House, Affiliated Lecturer in the Faculty of Divinity, University of Cambridge, and Director of Studies in Philosophy, St Edmund's College, Cambridge.

Simon Sarmiento earned a degree in Industrial Management at the Massachusetts Institute of Technology. He retired from a career in the computer software industry in 2000 and has also worked as a freelance journalist. In 2003 he was one of the founders of the 'Thinking Anglicans' website.

Jane Shaw is Dean for Religious Life and Professor of Religious Studies at Stanford. From 2010 to 2014, she was Dean of Grace Cathedral in San Francisco. She previously taught history and theology at the University of Oxford for sixteen years, was Dean of Divinity and Fellow of New College, Oxford, and was a theological consultant to the Church of England House of Bishops. She is the author and editor of several books on the history of Christianity. She is also Canon Emerita of Salisbury, where she served as the first Canon Theologian.

Alan Wilson studied at St John's College, Cambridge, and Balliol College (for a doctorate on modern historical theology) and Wycliffe Hall, Oxford. Since 2003, Alan has been the Bishop of Buckingham, in the Diocese of Oxford, where he has served since ordination in 1979. He is the chair of the Oxford Diocesan Board of Education and the author of *More Perfect Union? Understanding Same-Sex Marriage*.

Foreword

I try to be an evangelist at my local gym. The guys I work out alongside know I am a Christian and they are interested in spiritual things. I would love them to know God's amazing love in their lives but despite my best efforts they are not church attenders (yet!). When I talk to them about Church they ask me why the Church doesn't like people who are LGBT. My heart sinks, yet I know that many other people share that perspective.

Few issues have caused more controversy in the Church than the question of how we approach same-sex relationships. I was a youth worker in Northern Ireland during the peace process; there I learned the importance of reaching beyond the safety of our own comfort zone to ask why someone else holds a different view. We know Christians have different views on these matters, there are different views within different churches; the organisation I lead has a wide range of views. We need safe places for people to listen attentively to each other, to share together and to try to build trust and understanding. The Church of England's 'shared conversations' are designed to create such safe places and this book is a really helpful resource for these conversations.

As we discuss same sex relationships, of course we need to be faithful to Scripture and to discerning God's truth. But we also need to recognise that love and relationships are the holy ground of other people's lives. LGBT people are our friends, our family, they live in our communities, and they share our workplaces. This book is a resource that will stimulate and encourage us to form questions in a new way so we don't talk past each other or, worse, shout at each other. You may agree with the book or disagree with it, but it will help you consider how we can help LGBT people to know the Good News of Jesus Christ in their lives. I am grateful to Andrew and his colleagues for this new book and I commend it to you.

Canon Mark Russell
CEO Church Army
Member of the Archbishops' Council of the
Church of England
@markrusselluk

Chapter One

Being Followers of Jesus

As Christians, the most important thing about our identity is that we are 'in Christ' (2 Cor. 5.17), and the fundamental feature of our lives is that we are followers of Jesus. Everything we do is a response to him and what he has done for us. The goal of our lives is to 'run with perseverance the race that is set before us, looking to Jesus the pioneer and perfecter of our faith' (Heb. 12:1-2).[1]

Jesus came so that we can 'have life and have it abundantly' (John 10:10). His whole life shows us what that abundant life looks like. He brings healing, reconciliation, and joy to ordinary, sinful human beings, not least to people on the very edge of society. Jesus's love is also tough. He showed up, for instance, the ways in which religious leaders failed to live by what they preached. He disturbed people whose privileged position in society made them comfortable.

We follow Jesus, and that shapes everything: what we do, what we say, and how we pray. It shapes how we use our gifts, our time, and the things we own. It should also change the way we treat other people. That's what we want for this book – for ourselves, as authors, and for our readers – that it may help us think about how

1

we live and relate to others, as followers of Christ. We want to be faithful followers of God, whose name is Love (1 John 4:8).

Paying attention to one another

Part of what love demands of us is genuine, attentive listening. The conversations about sexuality that have been taking place in the Church of England, region by region, are one example of that listening process. That is the context for us writing this book, but we hope that it will be of use further afield too. It is good that the Church, and Christians across the country, are listening to the testimony of faithful Christians who describe their experiences of being lesbian, gay or bisexual. Listening and loving are a daily part of being a Christian, as is coming to a deeper understanding of one another, and of what it means to be a human being.[2]

To listen in love is not in the first place about wanting to change the other person, or about preparing to give an 'answer'. We listen, first of all, in order to understand. Through that, we gain some insight into the other person as a unique person, made in the image of God.

We have these conversations as much for our own sake as for others. To understand ourselves in relation to Jesus we need to understand both him and ourselves as best we can. In a book about sexuality, that will involve understanding the whole of ourselves in God's light. Coming to terms with ourselves as sexual persons, with all that this involves, is rarely an easy task. It is, however, an important aspect of human development and of Christian discipleship. Part of what the discussions within the Church offer is recognition that sexuality doesn't just concern other people, and their standing before God: it's about each of us, and our relation to Christ.

All teenagers, and indeed many adults, are likely to experience some anxiety over their sexual identity. However, it is still the case that heterosexual teenagers are unlikely to question their attraction to those of the opposite sex to the same degree that their lesbian, gay and bisexual peers will question their own desires. Society shapes its expectations around heterosexuality. Many people will 'grow up heterosexual' without reflecting on or struggling with that fact about their identity. By contrast, the testimonies of non-heterosexual Christians are often marked by profound struggle and personal courage.[3] This may be particularly evident in the case of those who, by force of circumstance or choice, find themselves 'coming out' quite publicly, often after years of anguish about whether to go public. We might think of the Evangelical Christian singer Vicky Beeching, who has spoken about her experience of isolation and fear, which is still widespread among gay, lesbian and bisexual Christians in many churches.[4] There are all too many examples of the damaging consequences of a Christian culture in which young gay and lesbian people either do not feel welcomed, or are not able to speak about themselves. In some cases these are deeply tragic, as one Christian couple and their vicar have very honestly and courageously acknowledged.[5] Even where the damage done to young people is not so profound, the effects of it can be lifelong.

Disagreement in good faith

It is easy to assume that there is a single, straightforward Christian view of particular controversial issues, but in the great majority of such cases, this is simply not true. The Church is a pilgrim Church, a community of people on a journey. It has always contained, and will always contain, a wide range of views, and Christians often disagree profoundly about important issues.

For example, Christians take different views of war. Some Christians are pacifists, believing that war is wrong under any circumstances. Others say that there can be a 'Just War': that sometimes war is necessary to prevent a greater evil. Yet people on all 'sides' in this debate acknowledge one another as fellow Christians, with different but sincerely-held views, resulting from prayerful consideration.

For some topics, the majority view among Christians has changed from one position, previously believed to be obviously 'biblical', to another. This happens when new insights lead people to apply Scripture to a particular situation in a new way. For example, slavery once seemed the obviously 'biblical' option, and early abolitionists faced strong 'biblical' opposition from fellow Christians. We will return to that below. What seems clear now — that what the abolitionist found in Scripture lined up far more closely with what we know about the just character of God — was not at all obvious to everyone at the time. Similarly, traditional teaching has changed as a result of new understandings or circumstances when it comes to lending money at interest and birth control (which we will also return to below).

There are of course many Christians who very sincerely believe that the Bible teaches that homosexuality is 'not part of God's plan'. Less frequently recounted are the perspectives of the many thoughtful, faithful Christians, who engage carefully with Scripture and have come to different conclusions. They have reached this position not as a result of ignoring the Bible, but because they are convinced that a faithful reading of the Bible points, instead, to treating same-sex relationships with value and support.

We acknowledge that many Christians do not feel able to join us in celebrating same-sex relationships in this way. We want to treat these Christians, who disagree with us, as sisters and brothers. We do also want to stress, however, that we can differ from them about homosexuality without being 'extreme liberals'. Many leading advocates of blessing for same-sex relationships are really quite conservative theologians – especially those working in Christian doctrine and philosophical theology – who do not think that rejecting gay and lesbian sexual relationships fits in with an integrated theological vision of the world.

The plain fact of the matter is that it is possible to take a very positive view of love between gay people and believe in the bodily resurrection of Jesus. Similarly, you can be glad when a lesbian friend finds someone to commit herself to – giving her whole self, including her body – and believe exactly what the Thirty-Nine Articles say about God.[6]

Being sinners

Part of our commitment to the historical faith of the Church is acknowledging that we all get things wrong: we are all sinners. The further we go on our journey with Christ, the more aware we are of this. As Paul reminds us, 'all have fallen short of the glory of God'(Rom. 3:22-23). Erring is an engrained aspect of our condition, and that is just as true – no more and no less – when it comes to sexuality and relationships.

We know that human sexual drives are strong, and can easily lead people off course. Sex isn't sinful in itself, nor is desire sinful in itself, but we can sin in this part of life, as in others. That's one reason why supportive institutions matter: we tend to need all the help we can get.[7] In fact, that's part of why we want the Church to bring same-sex relationships into its pastoral fold, and to bless them. It would be part of recognizing, publicly, that human commitment takes effort, and that we could all do with the guidance, prayer and support of the Christian family.

Paying attention to reality

This is a book about how to treat people well, and to behave morally ourselves. Questions like that are central to Christian thought, and always have been. The moral task – put simply – is to follow what's right, and avoid what's wrong. That's obvious enough. What's not always so obvious – but it's important – is that this involves paying attention to what things are *really like*. Christian ethics points us towards living in the way that's right for a human being. It's about being in harmony with the reality that God made. In that way, Christian ethics should always be a lively and engaging thing, and properly part of the good news that we share.[8]

Christian theology isn't a set of isolated, stand-alone ideas: it's a closely woven tapestry of truths that relate to the God who is eternal, creator, protector, redeemer, sanctifier, and our goal and final delight. Christian moral insights don't stand alone. They connect to that big theological picture at many different points.

One of the most important interconnections is that the God who *teaches* us is the same God who *made* us, and God loves what he made. Certainly, God's people sometimes wander, and God has to call us back. But even in our wandering state, God's commands are not burdensome or arbitrary. They are all about helping us to live more fully, to be what we were made to be. Nothing about how God speaks to us is mere whim; nothing about what God wants for us is random, nothing is plucked out of a hat. What God has done in creation, what God teaches us now, and what God promises for the future are all of a piece: they all join up, linked together in God's unchanging wisdom.

That might sound like an abstract point, but it matters practically, because it urges us to take seriously the work (sometimes difficult) of attending to what things are really like. It also suggests that if one thing we think God is saying about humanity conflicts with another thing we think God is saying, then all is not well with our big picture. One such conflict might be to think that love is central, and that it is generally not good that human beings should be alone (Gen. 2:18), but also to hear voices from the tradition standing against loving relationships for gay and lesbian men and women. Similarly, to take another example, the theological vision that sees God's work as all of one piece will urge us to take science seriously, as part of our moral deliberations.

There is an illustration for all of this in the English word 'good', with its three different but related meanings: to be 'good' means to be *moral*, to be *beneficial*, and to be *excellent*. We might say that a person is good ('She is moral'), or that exercise is good for you ('It is beneficial'), or that a painting is good ('It is an excellent painting'). These three meanings overlap. What it means for us to be *moral* is also what it means for us to do what's *good for us*, and to live in a way that fulfils us, which is to say that helps us be *excellent at being human*.[9]

Goodness of every kind comes from God, who is the ultimate source of all that is good (James 1:17). Similarly, God is the ultimate source of all truth, since God is Truth Itself.[10] Because of that, Christians never need fear the truth, or goodness, wherever they may find it: if it is true or good it comes from God. In moral matters, that urges us to have our eyes open. Christian ethics needs to pay fearless attention to the reality of things. It's not that we'll find the whole of what we need for our ethical perspective by looking at the world, of course not. But what God has spoken in the Bible relates to the world that God also spoke into being. No divine word of moral instruction is at cross-purposes with God's creative Word, who holds all things in existence, and gives them the gift of being what they are. That's why science is important. Certainly, science doesn't tell us everything we need to know. It doesn't replace God's revelation. It does bear witness, though, to the one who made all things, and it helps us to understand what they are like.

The work of Augustine of Hippo (354–430) is a cornerstone of Western theology. He was as much honoured after the Reformation as before. Augustine was aware of the need for Christians to be clear about facts, and to look reality in the face. He insisted on the hard work of paying attention to how things really are. What we would now call natural science (which is significant for the topic of this book) plays a part here, as Augustine saw.

> Usually, even a non-Christian knows something about the earth, the heavens, and the other elements of this world, about the motion and orbit of the stars and even their size and relative positions, about the predictable eclipses of the sun and moon, the cycles of the years and the seasons, about the kinds of animals, shrubs, stones, and so forth, and this knowledge he holds to as being certain from reason and experience. Now, it is a disgraceful and dangerous thing for a non-believer to hear a Christian, presumably giving the meaning of Holy Scripture, talking nonsense on these topics; and we should take all means to prevent such an embarrassing situation, in which people show up vast ignorance in a Christian and laugh it to scorn.[11]

Augustine's warning has stood the test of time. Truth does not contradict truth, nor goodness contradict goodness. Christian ethics isn't an arbitrary set of rules or a game about words: it's a description of reality. It matters for Christian ethics not to be ignorant of all that we can know from science about the reality of things. We turn to science in the next chapter. Augustine's comments are also all about mission, which is where this book will end. We would lose credibility in mission if we still proclaimed that the world was made in six twenty-four hour long days. We risk looking foolish if we talk about same-sex attraction and relationships without paying attention to the full range of what there is to know on that score.

When we want to think morally, when we want to bring all the riches of the Bible and the theological tradition to bear on some particular matter, it's our responsibility to *understand* what we are talking about as best we can. We might take the example of an ethical question about some new procedure in medicine. We can't give a properly Christian response until we know exactly what we're talking about. Or is there a question in economics? We would also have a duty to speak about that in an informed way.

The Bible, and the theology it has given birth to, are an inexhaustible source of wisdom. They touch on *everything*. Whatever we want to know about how to live, we find guidance there. We shouldn't think, though, that this divine gift exempts us from trying to understand a particular question or topic, as best we can, on its own terms. In fact, the better we understand the question we are asking, the more we'll get from thinking about it theologically. That would be the case, for instance, if we were thinking about how to live in light of some technological development, and it's the case when we think theologically about homosexuality: we have no reason to be afraid of learning what we can about that topic, as part of what it means to think about it theologically and in relation to the Bible.

That sets us up for the next chapter. Christians in the past *have* argued that sexual relationships between two men or two women, even in faithful, committed, life-long relationships (if they ever thought that such relationships could exist), are not good. They've said that they are not *morally* good, in part, because they've thought that they weren't good in those other two senses of that word: not *beneficial* (not 'good for' people) and not *excellent* (not examples of a certain sort of person living out their humanity in an excellent way). It's right to be concerned with what is beneficial and excellent for people. We agree with that. The difference is that we are convinced that gay and lesbian relationships *can* be very good for people, and that they *can* be all about people living in the ways Christian theology has long marked out as excellent (or 'virtuous'): as wise, courageous, temperate, just, hopeful, faithful, and loving.[12]

Chapter Two

Being Human

In this chapter we will look at what is known about same-sex attraction, and about sexual orientation and identity more generally. That will mean looking at biology and psychology. As we said in the previous chapter, living as Christians means caring deeply about the reality of things.

Without a doubt, human sexuality is a complex subject to study. Even so, the evidence is conclusive on at least three points: that human sexuality is diverse, that sexual orientation – whether heterosexual, homosexual, or bisexual – is not consciously chosen, and that, for the vast majority of people, sexual orientation is not easily changed.

Sexuality is complex

Human sexuality is an important, and complex, dimension of what it means to be a unique human being, created in the image of God. Thinking about it reminds us that only God really knows us fully (Ps. 139:1; 1 Cor. 13:12). Sexuality is complex because it involves our minds and our bodies, our selves and our behaviour towards others, what we think about ourselves and what others think about us. It touches on some of the most profound aspects of life, such as our capacity for intimacy, love and fidelity. Our sexual identity is hard to fathom because we might not always be conscious of the psychological processes that shape it. Sexuality is also complex because we are social beings, situated in a particular time, place, and culture. Our experiences, and how we interpret them, are shaped by shared social understandings and meanings, some of which we might be aware of consciously, and others not. Part of a Christian moral task is to become aware of those assumptions and to recognise that they are always in play, even when we reach to say the simplest things, such as that 'the Bible says ...' or 'the tradition says ...'.

The language of 'sexual orientation' is an important part of how we understand human identity, but as important phrases go, it is relatively new.[13] The previous assumption – discounted today – was that human beings are all fundamentally attracted to people of the opposite sex (and therefore also likely to be able to 'settle down' with someone of the opposite sex). The relatively recent concept of sexual orientation recognises that the situation is more complex than that, as the even more recent phenomenon of publicly acknowledged monogamous relationships between two people of the same sex also shows. Both of those developments are part of a bigger picture of changes within personal relationships over a longer time scale. Those changes include a more egalitarian or 'companionate' approach to marriage, and a less sharp distinction between the roles of men and women. Crucial to each of these changes is another very important shift, that whereas women and men previously operated in largely separate worlds, today they mix in almost every sphere of life.

The way in which many debates around sexuality are conducted shows that this complexity and mystery is easily forgotten. In particular, there's a temptation to reduce what should be a rounded ethical debate – involving the whole of what it means to be human and to love others – to a simple discussion of genital contact, as if that were all that sexuality were really about. There is a real problem with *Christians* talking about sexual relationships in this way, not least because that so easily simply mirrors, within the Church, a reductive, materialistic approach to sexuality, which we would rightly object to in the secular world. The Christian tradition, right from the Bible as its foundation, places its emphasis on relationships that belong within a wider community, looking outwards to others, and on the twin commandments to love God and neighbour as the touchstone for everything about the Christian life, including its sexual aspects.

Some may argue that particular sexual acts are wrong, with the conclusion that any intimacy between people of the same-sex must be condemned on that basis.[14] However, to reiterate that point, there is more to sexual relationships than isolated 'sexual acts', and if sex between two people counts as no more than 'a sexual act', something is amiss. The Christian tradition already stands out against such reductionism, not least when it says that our sexual orientation or identity cannot define us: it is only a part of who we are. The primary identity of any Christian is his or her identity 'in Christ', based on our common baptism into his Body. If we stand out against reductionism, we should be careful not to embrace it in the assumption that sexuality means no more than 'sexual acts'.

Changing scientific understanding

Christian understanding of aspects of human sexuality has changed over time, not least as part of our growing understanding of the natural world. For example, when it comes to animal reproduction, it was once widely thought that a woman was basically the 'field' into which the male 'seed' was planted, and that this seed already contained all that was necessary for human life.[15] Christians who took this view therefore ranked male masturbation close to murder,[16] and they considered it to be even more fundamentally against the order of nature than rape or incest, for instance.[17] However, when people discovered, through scientific enquiry, that this understanding of reproduction was incorrect, the ethical view of many Christians changed accordingly: murder is wrong, it's just that it doesn't bear upon the question of masturbation.

In ways like this, our understanding of human reproduction and sexuality has evolved. Thinking about same-sex attraction is part of that. The common assumption used to be that people who are attracted to others of the same sex are abnormal, in the sense that they suffer from a psychiatric condition: homosexuality was understood as a mental illness. We assumed that homosexuality, as a broad category of outlook, behaviour, and association, was in itself 'unhealthy', and associated with other physical or medical problems. However, the more work was done to examine the actual lives and well-being of gay and lesbian people, the shakier that conviction became.

By 1973, when homosexuality stopped being classified as a mental illness in the United Kingdom, the scientific and medical consensus had changed entirely. The previous view, of homosexuality as an illness, had been recognised not just as false, but as extremely damaging. The medical opinion on this is rock solid. Homosexuality is not damaging to people; it is the assumption that it is 'unhealthy' that damages them.

This is important for our discussion on several levels, not least because – as we saw in the previous chapter – Christian ethics has a strong interest in what is natural and healthy for people. The older picture assumed that everyone is 'naturally' attracted to people of the opposite sex, but that some individuals choose to go against these natural inclinations in order to have sexual relationships with people of the same sex. That particular vision of nature leads to a particular vision of ethics. In that context, it's unsurprising that homosexual activity was viewed as harmful, both to the individuals involved and to society as a whole. It was seen as unnatural, perverse, and going against the grain of how the world should be.

Today, this is no longer our best scientific understanding of homosexuality. Clear, robust evidence shows that, for some people, same-sex attraction is natural, inevitable, and beyond their conscious control. As twenty-first-century Christians, rejoicing in our God-given reason, this relatively new scientific picture needs to inform our Christian response to same-sex attraction.

To appreciate what the science shows us, it is helpful to consider two significant developments. One is our better understanding of the importance of emotional and relational aspects of sexuality. The other is our greater sense of the diversity of human experience.

Emotional intimacy

Developments in psychology have shown that sexuality is part of the complex relation of what makes us who we are — weaving together emotion, self-understanding, and behaviour — which develops from infancy onwards. How that develops has a profound impact on our ability to form successful relationships with others, especially intimate relationships. 'Success' and difficulty here cut across distinctions of sexuality: gay or straight, for some people developing a healthy sexual relationship comes easily, for others it does not.

Psychologists are now able to say more clearly what the characteristics of an emotionally healthy intimate relationship are. Those who are considered emotionally 'mature' would be those who can commit to a particular person, in a relationship that lasts over time, and who can meet the demands for change that come with any relationship, in ways which do not compromise personal integrity but develop it.[18] In this framework, promiscuity, for example, would be regarded as psychologically dysfunctional, while a stable and committed relationship is seen as the mature and healthy course for life. This lines up closely with a Christian ethical approach, which sees permanent, faithful, stable marriage as the ideal.

Drawing on this relatively recent psychological understanding, the Christian ethicist Margaret Farley has identified several closely related guiding principles to determine whether sexual behaviour within a relationship is right or just. These include the avoidance of betrayal or deceit; free consent – the absence of coercion or violence; a commitment to mutuality, which involves both partners in a free giving and receiving; equality between partners; a commitment of time, but also a commitment to equality, mutuality, and justice;

fruitfulness – that loving sexual relationships should promote love, hospitality, and inclusion for others within the community; and social justice, that is, not treating others instrumentally as a way to get what we want.[19]

These are the psychological facts, which a Christian will no doubt recognise as profoundly in tune with the Christian ethical vision. In these vital terms, there is nothing 'unnatural' about the psychology of same-sex relationships. It is clear that a great many same-sex couples embody these principles (although some do not); just as a great many heterosexual couples do (although some do not). A person in a relationship with someone of the same sex is just as capable of emotional intimacy and personal integrity as a person in a relationship with someone of the opposite sex.[20]

That is a crucial part of the new situation in which the Church finds itself when it comes to same-sex relationships. As social acceptance has grown, so has awareness of the many examples of gay and lesbian people in committed and faithful relationships. As more and more of us know people in a relationship like that it has also become clear that, like their heterosexual equivalents, such relationships can and do demonstrate the qualities we seek, not least in marriage. We encounter in gay and lesbian relationships the same sort of virtues that we pray for in the marriage service: love, trust, joy, commitment, unity, loyalty, growth, and mutual support.

Coming to understand this psychological reality is what led many national and international psychological bodies to remove homosexuality from the list of mental illnesses. That same, developed understanding of the psychological dimension of sexuality must now also affect how Christians approach the ethical dimension of the issue.

Diversity is natural

We are all different. Being different from one another is part of being human. Variation is a natural biological phenomenon, and an important part of the human condition. We are different in all sorts of ways, some physical (height, eye colour, predisposition to particular diseases), some mental (intelligence, musical aptitude), and some in our temperament (extroversion or introversion, impulsiveness). It is part of human nature for human beings to be different.

The impact of some of these differences depends on the society in which we live. For example, poor eyesight would have been disastrous in early hunter-gatherer societies, but is a minor and easily corrected inconvenience in modern western society. Sometimes moral judgements are made according to particular characteristics, such as skin colour or left-handedness. These distinctions and judgements have often led to practices we would now consider discriminatory and harmful.

Part of the extent and depth of this diversity is natural variation in the bodily way in which we are sexual beings. In terms of sexual anatomy, there are a number of rare, but well-documented, variations in sexual development (often referred to as 'intersex'). In such cases, people may have bodies that are neither typically male nor female. There may be a contrast between the sex suggested by their chromosomes and internal organs, and their external appearance, or they may have ambiguous genitalia.[21] Although there are relatively few intersex people, as Christians we believe that *all* people are made in the image of God, and so it is important to take the example and experience of these individuals into account too.

There is also variation in people's experience of erotic attraction, including same-sex dimension. There is strong evidence that sexual activity between people of the same sex is found in all contemporary cultures and, as far as we can know, throughout history.[22] This has been clear to anthropologists for well over sixty years. It indicates that same-sex desire is part of the variety of human experience and constitution.[23]

A spectrum of desire

Over the course of the twentieth century, the human sciences clearly established that human sexuality exists on a spectrum. The majority of the population is attracted exclusively to the opposite sex. A small proportion of the population is attracted exclusively to people of the same sex. Another (larger) group is attracted to people of both sexes. In short, it is now commonly agreed that for a significant minority of the population, attraction to people of the same sex is part of who they are, and part of the natural function of human life for them. Just as a sizeable minority of people is naturally left handed, so some people are attracted to people of the same sex.

An approach to sexuality in terms of a spectrum was pioneered by Alfred Kinsey (1894-1956), following an extensive study of the sexual desires and self-identity of men and women. Kinsey proposed that each person could be placed on a spectrum, where 0 is exclusively heterosexual, and 6 is exclusively homosexual. Someone recorded as a 3 would be equally attracted to men and women. This approach may seem simplistic, but it has proved to be a robust way of describing human diversity, and has been the basis of subsequent research.

Analysis of what this research shows varies significantly, but a recent review of eleven independent studies found that around 3.5% of people identify as lesbian, gay or bisexual. Of those, around half are bisexual. Women are more likely to see themselves as bisexual than men, and men are more likely to identify as exclusively homosexual than women. In addition, around 8% of the population report that they have at some point engaged in sexual activity with someone of the same sex. Around 11% report that they have experienced same-sex attraction at some point in their lives.[24]

Biological angles

As we might expect, scientists have been interested in the wider scientific picture around sexual attraction. As with opposite-sex attraction, there is clear evidence that some men and women are biologically predisposed to be attracted to people of the same sex as them. This evidence includes the observation that homosexuality is found widely across human societies, and that sexual preference is not consciously chosen by people (which is an observation that the heterosexual reader might also quite readily be able to confirm). In addition, there is extensive evidence for same-sex sexual activity in many hundreds of animal species, including a large number of mammals.[25] Clearly, one should be careful in drawing simplistic or specific conclusions from this evidence. Nevertheless, it does provide broad support for the proposition that a predisposition to homosexual (and heterosexual) desire and activity has a biological cause.

A fuller biological understanding of any aspect of being human calls for exploration of the causes that lie behind it (a genetic cause, for example), as well as an account of how that cause influences development in the way that it does. Working out how to study a complex aspect of human behavior, such as sexuality, is very challenging, and there are many pitfalls in designing studies and interpreting the results.

For a start, scientists themselves might question whether the most important biological distinction to be made within human sexuality is the gender of the person to whom one is attracted.[26] This is far from clear. We can study sexuality in terms of gender, but that is only part of a much wider picture. Scientific studies also need to be cautious about supposing that homosexuality (or indeed heterosexuality) is a uniform phenomenon: that at some level all homosexuals (or heterosexuals) are the same. Even recent studies sometimes conflate lesbian and gay populations into one, when it is highly unlikely that the underlying biological processes are the same in those two broad cases. A third factor is that the search for the '*causes* of homosexual attraction' is being conducted against the backdrop of what is still quite a limited understanding of the development of sexuality. For example, we have very little idea of when or how sexual identity (the internal mental state) is established.

As a result, it's considerably clearer to see *that* causes are at work than it is to discern exactly *what* those causes are, and how they work together. That a proportion of the population is attracted more or less exclusively to people of the same sex, and that this attraction cannot be changed, is clear. *How* that attraction is established causally, or how opposite-sex attraction is established for that matter, is less clear. Generally, enquiries follow two lines, which are not mutually exclusive:

first, that some people have a genetic predisposition to same-sex attraction, and, secondly that brains develop along a particular path (as more heterosexual or more homosexual) as a consequence of particular patterns in their exposure to hormones in the womb.

Genes and Development

In thinking about genetics, we must start with a note of caution. The idea of a 'gay gene', or indeed of a 'straight gene', simply doesn't make sense to a serious scientist, for a number of reasons. First, and most importantly, very few human traits are genetically determined in a direct way by just one gene, or even by just a few. Then there are all the 'environmental factors' that people encounter – everything that comes their way from the womb onwards – which constantly interact with the play of our genes. As an example of how important those 'outside factors' are, consider how our immune system develops through its contact with the bacteria that we encounter. Without interactions with germs, even a perfectly 'healthy' set of genes would not give us a healthy immune system. The alliteration of 'nature versus nurture' might lend itself to a neat division between the effects of internal genes and external influences, but such a division is woefully simplistic.[27]

The way in which our genes leave their stamp on us is an incredibly dynamic process: they shape who we are only as part of a long, elaborate process of development. That process starts in the womb, and carries on outside it, and it's as much about *when* a particular gene has an effect, and when it doesn't, as anything else. It is also about how one gene affects another. If we have achieved any clarity in the genetics of development, it is clarity about how immensely complex that picture is. If there is a significant genetic component to sexual orientation, it will involve the interaction of a number of different genes, at various stages, with each other and with a range of environmental factors.

All this means that it's very difficult to distinguish the consequences of our genetic inheritance from the effects of social and environmental factors. Often the best we can do is to talk about varying degrees of biological 'influence' or 'predisposition'.[28]

All that said, there is quite strong evidence to suggest that variation in sexual attraction has a genetic component. This has consistently been the finding of the best scientific evidence available, including studies involving families and twins. In family studies, higher than average rates of homosexuality within families are investigated; in twin studies, we compare rates of homosexuality in identical and non-identical twins. Both approaches produce results that are consistent with genetic influence.

Quantitative attempts to 'assess' the genetic component of complex human attributes in numerical terms are fraught with interpretative difficulty, and the results from individual studies can vary significantly. Nevertheless, one of the most rigorous twin studies, based on 4,901 participants, estimated a heritability factor of 50-60% for women and 30% for men.[29] (A heritability measure is an estimate of the proportion of the variation that exists within a particular population than can be ascribed to genetic influence). To put this into context, estimates for complex human behaviours very rarely exceed 50%. That said, genetic studies to date have not provided much of a clue as to *how* genes might influence the development and variety of sexuality. The human processes we are talking about here – about psychology and its biological foundations – are so complex that we should not hold out a great deal of hope that genetic studies will tell us much more about mechanisms any time soon. They do, however, support the clear consensus that there is some biological influence involved in sexual orientation.[30]

The other factor that we mentioned may be important is the environment we experience in the womb. In the complex process of sexual differentiation, the period in the womb is easily the most important, where the foetus develops in response to a range of pre-natal hormones during key stages of brain development. Extensive tests on animals show that there is a critical time before birth when patterns of hormonal and brain development are determined for the rest of life. These animal studies, involving a variety of species, also show evidence that patterns of sexual attraction are influenced during this stage of development. It would of course be unethical to conduct this sort of experiment on humans. Nevertheless there is some evidence of differences in brain structures between heterosexual and homosexual people. Such differences in brain structure seem to occur during the development of the foetus in the uterus as a result either of the direct influence of genes or of pre-natal hormones.[31]

The biological factors that are at work in forming someone as homosexual (or indeed, as heterosexual) remain, to some extent, a mystery, and that includes questions about the relative roles of genetics and experiences in early development. What is clear is that scientists agree almost universally that there is a biological basis to same-sex attraction.

Determined and chosen

For many people thinking ethically about homosexuality, it matters whether sexual attraction is hard-wired. The facts on that score do not settle anything – we still need to think about how those sorts of observations play out in ethical thinking – but we can hardly ignore them: not responsibly anyway. Two issues seem to be particularly at stake: whether or not someone's sexuality can change, and to what extent someone's sexuality is a choice.

Those questions relate to the evidence for genetic factors, but more is involved than that. Genetic factors aren't the only reason why someone might have a disposition that can't be changed. Any number of influences may result in something that is hard to change about who we are, and that may indeed be unchangeable. Those influences include the particular environment of the mother's womb, as we have seen, and all sorts of things that come our way later on.

However, whatever the causes, we know that for the vast majority of people who are attracted to people of the same sex, that attraction cannot be changed: not by them, and not by anyone else. We know this, not least, because of a terrible legacy of experiments on gay men in the twentieth century. For decades, especially after World War II, all sorts of techniques were tried, including chemical castration, and horrific aversion techniques involving electric shocks and nausea-inducing drugs. Many methods were tried, but they didn't change their 'patient's' sexual orientation. If we want to see why there is such sympathy towards gay people today, we need look no further than this. The most famous example of treating someone this way is the code-breaking mathematical hero of the Second World War, Alan Turing (1912-1954). It is widely regarded as having pushed him to suicide, although not before he had played his role in shaping the outcome of the War.[32]

None of these terrible interventions – attempting to be a 'cure' – make sense outside of a scheme in which homosexuality is seen as an illness. For decades, in an era when that assumption prevailed, these experiments produced no evidence of 'successful' treatment, and often left people deeply damaged. Happily, in Western society today, gay, lesbian, and bisexual people no longer live in fear of medical experimentation of this sort, and homosexuality was removed from the World Health Organization list of mental disorders in 1990.

Today, indeed, even the use of counselling techniques in an attempt to change someone's sexual orientation is widely discredited, and receives no support from the relevant professional bodies. Those few individuals who still support such interventions only report 'success' in a small minority of cases. Meanwhile, these 'treatments' continue to cause harm,[33] and the climate of non-acceptance to which they belong has done great damage.

Some conservative religious groups continue to hold the view that unwanted same-sex attraction can be changed through 'conversion therapy' (and that such attraction *should* be unwanted): through prayer and various forms of counselling. However, even that conviction is changing. One of the most prominent 'ex-gay' Christian organizations, *Exodus International*, demonstrated significant courage and humility in publicly renouncing this position, and they apologised for the hurt it had caused.[34] Their experience was that attempts to change people's sexual orientation very often simply did not produce the outcome they wanted, and that these attempts were frequently harmful.

This brings us back to the question of choice. The evidence from psychology and the biological sciences is that someone's sexual attraction – his or her orientation – is in-built, not chosen (and, as we saw, that it can rarely be changed). All the same, an unchosen *disposition* does not prevent us from choosing in another sense: however strongly influenced we are by our predispositions, or by other factors, we all have a choice about how to *act*. Powerful feelings of attraction may be inevitable, but how they translate into behaviour remains a matter of choice. Strong biological influences do not remove the moral responsibility of the individual. Nor, on the other hand, can we simply dismiss what we know about the human constitution, as if that were irrelevant to our ethical thinking, nor ignore the ways in which sexual desire, and possibilities for committed sexual relationships, exist for lesbian, gay, and bisexual people.[35]

This is a book about some ethical questions, and an important part of ethics is to guide us in this realm of choice. The heterosexual Christian starts off from a particular position. She is a sexual being, and that's an important part of who she is: of who God has made her to be. This touches on all sorts of aspects of her life. As part of that she has certain hopes and desires: for companionship, for intimacy, for support, for a relationship where she learns to live beyond her own sometimes selfish ego, for nurturing children, for belonging to a family unit that contributes to the wider community. She *might*, perhaps, discern a vocation to celibacy, but most likely not: that sense of calling seems only to apply to a small minority of people. Most likely, she thinks that those hopes and desires will be fulfilled in a sexual relationship. Being a Christian, she wants her choices to be informed by what the Christian tradition says about these matters: about companionship, intimacy, support, overcoming selfishness, forming a family and being active in the community, and so on. She wants to find someone to whom she can make a life-long commitment, before God and the Church.

The homosexual Christian finds herself in the same position. Her sexuality, too, touches upon the whole of her life; she too has certain hopes and desires. The findings of contemporary biology and psychology show us that the attractions she feels are part of who she is, as they would be for her heterosexual sister, and that the hopes and desires that belong alongside it are also the same: they are for companionship, intimacy and support, for a relationship where she learns to live beyond her ego, forming a family, and being active in the community.[36] The homosexual Christian *might* discern a vocation to celibacy, but if it is a true vocation it will be one that makes sense of who she is – and not a matter of running away from it – and we have no reason in advance to suppose that the gay Christian will be able to say that celibacy is what she was made for, any more than the average straight Christian will say that. She has choices to make. Just as with her straight sister, they are genuine choices. She is not compelled by her sexuality. But again, just as with a heterosexual Christian, those choices are made in relation to who she is and what her hopes and desires might reasonably be. Most likely, she wants to find someone to whom she can make a life-long commitment, before God and the Church.

Conclusion

It is clear that our scientific understanding of homosexuality and same-sex desire has changed profoundly in the past one hundred years or so. There is a clear consensus within the medical profession, and among psychologists, that the strong feelings of sexual attraction and desire towards those of the same sex experienced by a small but significant proportion of the population is entirely natural to them: it is entirely equivalent to the way that others experience sexual desire for people of the opposite sex. Research also shows that when such feelings find sexual expression within committed, romantic relationships they do not cause harm either to the people themselves or to others but, like heterosexual relationships, that this can be a source of comfort, joy and fruitfulness.

While the biological basis of homosexuality is not known in any real detail, all the evidence points towards some genetic predisposition, though it is likely that pre-natal hormones and other factors may also play a role. The suggestion that homosexuality is an 'illness' of some kind has been thoroughly discredited.

The sciences can never provide a 'trump card' in ethical discussions. However, new discoveries and understandings can and do shift the background against which well-informed ethical thinking takes place.

Chapter Three

Being Biblical

At this point some readers may well be thinking, 'That's all well and good, but it does not change what the Bible clearly says. I am truly sorry for the difficulty faced by people with same-sex attraction, even if it is "natural", but the Bible says that same-sex relationships are prohibited. Full stop.' In this chapter we turn to think about the Bible, and about how it features in our Christian discipleship, because attention to the authority and inspiration of the Bible is clearly part of what it means for us to be followers of Jesus: indeed, attention to the Bible is one of the main ways we know *how* to follow him.

Just as there are people who set out opposition to same-sex relationships in this way, others express their support for same-sex relationships in terms of overcoming 'errors' in the Bible. They may think that the biblical writers *must* be wrong about same-sex relationships because of the time and context in which they were writing. If that were true, we would have to understand sexuality and marriage by drawing upon other sources, discounting the Bible. That is not a line of argument we wish to pursue. Instead, like many Christians, we have found that a journey towards support for committed same-sex relationships has not been a journey away from the Bible, but a journey that involves *taking the Bible seriously*.

We disagree with people from a more traditionalist perspective, if they think that the core problem in our disagreements about sexuality is that Christians on the other side of the debate simply do not take the Bible seriously enough. We also disagree with people who, from a more liberal perspective, think that the core problem is that other Christians take the Bible far too seriously. Rather, we would say, the problem is that *none* of us are, on the whole, taking the Bible seriously enough. Holy Scripture, inspired by God's Holy Spirit, and written, compiled and handed down by generations of the people of God, is central to Christian discipleship. We do not contest that claim.

What we *should* be willing to contest, though, is the sense that there is only one, settled, and unquestionable human understanding of precisely what the Bible says on a given issue, including this one. We have seen, throughout Christian history, that what previously seemed to have been stated with utter clarity in some parts of the Bible, can turn out to need understanding completely differently in relation to the Bible as a whole. What were thought to be *the* authoritative biblical texts on the matter can later be gathered within a wider whole. The same Holy Spirit who worked in the historical circumstances of the writing and preservation of Scripture continues to work. The Spirit leads people

– people who regard the Bible as authoritative *and continue to do so* – to see that they have been going against the greater biblical witness, and are therefore, unwittingly, undermining the Bible. Slavery, of course, is one of the most striking historical examples.

There is vastly more biblical material on slavery than there are passages about same-sex relations. Noah's son, Canaan, is made his brothers' slave (Gen. 9:25-27). Abraham owned slaves (Gen. 12:16), and God is described as blessing Abraham by giving him male and female slaves (Gen. 24:35). The leaders of God's people are often described as taking slaves at God's command (Joshua, David, Solomon – see for instance Joshua 9:3-27; 2 Sam. 20:24; 1 Kings 9:20-21, and see Judges 1:28), and Job insists he has treated his slaves with fairness (Job 31:13). The law has no problem with slavery: it is assumed in the Ten Commandments (Exodus 20:10, 17; Deut. 5:14, 21), and is explicitly affirmed in the law codes, which specify that slaves may be taken from amongst other nations and resident aliens, and that 'they may be your property' and 'a possession for your children after you, for them to inherit as property' (Lev. 25:44-45). There are many passages in the law and prophets that provide instruction in the fair treatment of slaves, with no indication that slavery itself is immoral or should be abolished.

Jesus is never recorded as condemning slavery, and slaves appear in Jesus' parables without questions being raised about the institution of slavery itself. The New

Testament epistles exhort slaves to remain in slavery and to obey their masters (1 Cor. 7:21; Col. 3:22).[37] It is assumed that some Christians will own slaves, and be slaves themselves. To them, this advice is addressed:

> Let all who are under the yoke of slavery regard their masters as worthy of honour, so that the name of God and the teaching may not be blasphemed. Those who have believing masters must not be disrespectful to them on the ground that they are members of the Church; rather they must serve them all the more, since those who benefit by their service are believers and beloved (1 Tim. 6:1-2).

When debate about slavery raged during the nineteenth century, for instance during the American Civil War, many Christians put forward *pro*-slavery arguments. Those arguments were often centred on this overwhelming biblical support for slavery. Christians in their own time, they thought, like Israelites and Christians of old, must follow Scripture and treat their slaves 'fairly' and 'justly', but no Bible-believing Christian, they thought, could say that there was anything un-Christian about *slavery itself*.

Biblical support for slavery was absolutely self-evident to these Christians, and to millions of Christians in the centuries preceding theirs. Slavery was not defeated until Christians began to speak about the overarching witness of Scripture as a whole, which clearly opposes inequality, oppression, domination, and abuse. Slavery was not defeated until Christians recognised that Jesus Christ, presented to us in the Bible, is the one who frees slaves and makes everyone brothers and sisters, and that following Jesus must require the same. In a particularly eloquent sermon, Henry Ward Beecher (1813-1887) questioned how the same Bible that proclaims this Jesus could be used to defend slavery:

> 'I came to open the prison-doors', said Christ; and that is the text on which men justify shutting them and locking them. 'I came to loose those that are bound'; and that is the text out of which men spin cords to bind men, women, and children. 'I came to carry light to them that are in darkness and deliverance to the oppressed'; and that is the Book from out of which they argue, with amazing ingenuity, all the infernal meshes and snares by which to keep men in bondage. It is pitiful.[38]

The Bible clearly assumes the validity of slavery, yet the overarching message of Scripture as it unfolds requires that we reject slavery: God is the one who calls a people by freeing them from slavery, Jesus is the one who comes to set captives free, and the Church is the body by which he tears down the walls that prevent everyone from participating equally in the good news (Eph. 2:11-22). It took time – far too much time – for Christians to connect their understanding of the good news with their views on slavery.[39]

One lesson to take from this is that part of taking the Bible seriously must be to recognise that we cannot appreciate the whole of what it has to teach us in an easy and straightforward way, without errors of understanding – as if that were a light matter for finite and fallible human beings. Much less can we imagine that the God who inspired these texts, and inspires the Church today, can be contained in our limited understanding of Scripture. We must be open to the continuing movement of God, within the Church and out, to bring us into truth. That includes being willing to acknowledge that a particular understanding of some particular texts may be preventing us from seeing a broader truth that permeates the Bible as a whole. We will return to this dynamic of 'being part of the story' in the next chapter.

Just as some biblical writers assumed that slavery is acceptable, so some assumed (though in far fewer instances) that sex between two women or two men is unacceptable. We must consider this assumption carefully, taking it seriously, since asking about the theological and moral witness of 'Scripture overall' is not a recipe for ignoring particulars within the Bible. In the limited space of this chapter, we can only gesture towards interpretations of the most debated passages, and commend to readers the very fine and detailed work that others have done on these texts elsewhere.[40]

The limited space dedicated to those passages here does not mean that we think that anyone should 'dispense' with them. It does indicate, though, that those texts are not the only sentences in the Bible that matter in this conversation.

Some of the texts that are commonly brought into the debate about homosexuality in fact have little or no relevance to the topic in hand. This is especially true of the story of Sodom and Gomorrah. For centuries this narrative has been associated with homosexuality, and has given the words 'sodomy' and 'sodomite' to the English language. However, the narrative itself (Gen. 19) is not about same-sex relations.

The men of Sodom are described as coming to Lot's house and demanding that he surrender his visitors to them (these visitors are angels, although that is still hidden). Sodom is condemned and destroyed, along with surrounding cities. The book of Jude says that Sodom and Gomorrah 'indulged in sexual immorality and pursued unnatural lust' (Jude 7), which lends itself to the association of this story with homosexuality. However, if the narrative is indeed about sex, it is about an attempted gang rape perpetrated by a mob against two outsiders who are guests. It is difficult to make a case that the heart of the problem is same-sex relationships, and certainly not the sort of committed, monogamous same-sex relationship that many value today.

If there is any ambiguity left by the narrative in Genesis and Jude, the matter is made clear by Ezekiel:

'This was the guilt of your sister Sodom: she and her daughters had pride, excess of food, and prosperous ease, but did not aid the poor and needy. They were haughty, and did abominable things before me; therefore I removed them when I saw it' (Ezek. 16:49-50). We would not be taking the Bible seriously by continuing to interpret this narrative in a different way than the Bible itself does. Interpreters need to be honest: the association of the narrative with homosexuality comes primarily from centuries of overlaid interpretation, not from the way in which the Bible itself presents this story or reflects upon it.

Two passages in Leviticus are much less ambiguous. Leviticus 18:22 reads, 'You shall not lie with a male as with a woman; it is an abomination', and in Levitcus 20:13a we find, 'If a man lies with a male as with a woman, both of them have committed an abomination'. There is no question that these texts are referring to sexual acts between two men.

However, if the timeless truth and literal application of these verses is what is being insisted upon, we have troubles to address beyond homosexual intercourse. Chapter 18 treats sexual intercourse during menstruation with equal seriousness to incest and sex with animals. Why, we should surely ask, would we be happy to reconsider *that* as culturally determined, and irrelevant to practice today, but insist that the prohibition against men having sex with men is as timeless as the prohibitions against incest and bestiality?

By what criteria are we associating some parts with timelessness and others with cultural limitations? More seriously still, the prohibition in chapter 20 against sex between two men is followed with the penalty of death: the second half of the verse reads 'they shall be put to death, their blood is upon them'. Again, by what criteria are we to judge one half of this verse as timeless and the other half as irrelevant to our contemporary setting? Can we uphold the prohibition as timeless if we reject the prescribed penalty? Further still, can we uphold that prohibition if we do not treat with equal severity the other prohibitions in the same chapter, which also have the penalty of death, including the death penalty for 'all those who curse father or mother'?

So, while there is no question that these texts condemn sex between two men, there are many questions about how, or if, that prohibition should apply today, and about whether it is not to be interpreted in the same light as the many prohibitions in Leviticus against all manner of foods, practices and states, which were considered 'unclean' or otherwise forbidden then, but are unproblematic today.[41] The fact that the prohibitions stand only against sex between *men* pushes us even further towards the conclusion that this is a prohibition of something specific, to do with ritual law and uncleanness, instead of being a timeless, blanket statement about same-sex relationships.[42]

A similar question about timelessness versus culturally specific prohibitions arises in relation to two key New Testament verses, 1 Corinthians 6:9 (which includes *malakoi* and *arsenokoites* – 'male prostitutes' and 'sodomites' in the NRSV – in a list of wrongdoers who will not inherit the kingdom) and 1 Timothy 1:10 (which also includes *arsenokoites*, in a list of those who do not conform to the gospel). Intense debate continues to this day about the meaning of these two Greek words. Significantly, scholars have noted that translations of these words have differed a good deal over the centuries, with Christians often associating them with practices that were of particular concern at the time, such as masturbation, being effeminate, or homosexuality. There hasn't been an 'agreed interpretation' of what those words mean, such that it would suddenly now be called into question by 'revisionists'.[43]

Some more recent studies suggest that male prostitution and pederasty – sex between an adult man and a young boy – are the practices in question,[44] practices we would continue to denounce today: straightforwardly, and on the basis of a broad biblical and theological vision. But the truth is that there is little consensus about what these words mean. What it *does* seem safe to say, however, is that whatever in Greco-Roman culture is being condemned, it would not have been anything like the committed, long-term, same-sex partnerships that we are discussing in this book, simply because analogies did not exist at that time.

This brings us to the remaining two debated texts, which seem to be of a different order than those discussed thus far. Unlike the passages in Leviticus, and in those New Testament epistles, there seems to be less room for talking about these texts as culturally specific, making prohibitions either against things that we no longer consider 'unclean' or against practices that are not analogous to contemporary, committed same-sex relationships. The remaining two passages address the issue in a way which is much more fundamental, and much more about the created nature of human beings, and about what God intends for our relationships with one another. These are the creation accounts of Genesis 1 and 2, and the opening chapter of Romans.

In Genesis, God creates a man and a woman. In the first account (chapter 1), God creates man and woman together, in God's own image, and tells them to be fruitful and multiply. In the second account (chapter 2), God creates the man first, and then creates the woman to be his helper. The man recognises the woman as 'bone of my bones and flesh of my flesh', and it is said that '[t]herefore a man leaves his father and his mother and clings to his wife, and they become one flesh' (Gen. 2:23a and 24). Many have argued from these accounts that the relationship between one man and one woman is at the very heart of God's intentions for creation. This might be argued in terms of procreation: only a heterosexual couple can (naturally) reproduce ('be fruitful'). Or it may be argued in terms of complementarity: that men and women are different and need one another. Some would go so far as to say that human beings are only truly reflecting the image of God in the union of a man and a woman: heterosexual complementarity is required for us to be fully human as God intended. It is very difficult, however, to argue either of those points in relation to historic Christian tradition or contemporary Church practice.

That reference to 'fruitfulness' is one reason. From its earliest days the Church's theologians have argued that biological reproduction is not the only way to be fruitful, or even the most meaningful way. John Chrysostom (c. 349-407) is characteristic of the foundational period for Christian thought when he writes that procreation was commanded (in Genesis) before there was hope of resurrection in Christ. People had to have children in order to matter after death,

> But now that resurrection is at our gates, and we do not speak of death, but advance toward another life better than the present, the desire for posterity is superfluous. If you desire children, you can get much better children now, a nobler childbirth and better help in your old age, if you give birth by spiritual labour.[45]

Here, Chrysostom is simply following a line of argument begun by Paul in 1 Corinthians 7. The Church honours marriage, and bearing and raising children, but that does not exhaust the purpose of human life, or of marriage, for that matter: Christian Churches do not deny marriage to couples who cannot reproduce biologically, and that practice too has ancient roots.[46] Many heterosexual couples are infertile, and many others become couples after their childbearing years. We do not deny the validity of those relationships, or forbid them from consummating their marriages, just because of their inability to reproduce. Nor do Christians, not even those who keep to traditional Roman Catholic teaching forbidding contraception, require that all sexual acts must be potentially procreative.[47] If heterosexual couples are free to engage in sexual activities that we know cannot lead to procreation, how can we argue against same-sex intercourse on the grounds that it cannot lead to procreation? In the end, as Rowan Williams put it,

> In a Church that accepts the legitimacy of contraception, the absolute condemnation of same-sex relations of intimacy must rely either on an abstract fundamentalist deployment of a number of very ambiguous biblical texts, or on a problematic and nonscriptural theory about natural complementarity, applied narrowly and crudely to physical differentiation...[48]

Such 'crude' reduction of complementarity to 'physical differentiation' is not the only or best way to interpret the Genesis accounts. Nothing about how Adam and Eve complemented one another – genitally or otherwise

– is noted there. Instead, what *is* affirmed is that the man and the woman were both created in God's image Gen. 1:27). It is closer to the text, therefore, to argue for an understanding of human relationships, love, and intimacy based on the mutual recognition of another human being, as created and loved by God.[49]

Human love is an invitation for us to be caught up into the love of God. In our love for that other person, we encounter the love of God: God wills for the other person to be, and delights in him or her, and our love shares in that. Then, in that other person's recognition and love for us, we encounter a reflection of God loving us, and willing us to be. This two-fold participation in the love of God, through a mutual love between two people, underlies a Christian understanding of what love means, and not least of what sexual love means. No form of psychological or physical 'complementarity' is either ruled out or required by that account.

All the same, Christian arguments against same-sex relationships do often appeal to complementarity, if they claim that it is clearly 'natural' for men and women to complement one another, while it is 'unnatural' for men or women to attempt such complementarity with members of the same sex.[50] This brings us to Romans 1, in which the people are said to have become foolish and idolatrous, turning their backs on God, and so

> God gave them up to degrading passions. Their women exchanged natural intercourse for

unnatural, and in the same way also the men, giving up natural intercourse with women, were consumed with passion for one another. Men committed shameless acts with men and received in their own persons the due penalty for their error (Rom. 1:26-27).

In one sense this could not be clearer; it is a biblical condemnation of same-sex intercourse just as unquestionable as that in Leviticus. Yet many questions quickly emerge. We have already asked of the Leviticus verses how to decide what is timeless and what is culturally determined, and this remains a pertinent question with Paul (and to suppose that the Old Testament requires careful interpretation and attention to context, but that the New Testament does not, is decidedly odd).[51] For one thing, Paul is not actually primarily out to teach about sexuality here; he is setting the stage for a grand narrative about Jews and Gentiles.

Paul sets up that discussion by calling upon certain assumptions about sexuality: assumptions that he shared with his readers. It takes a conscious step on our part, therefore, to take this passage as teaching on the subject in a way that is fixed for all time.[52] Furthermore, the phrase translated 'unnatural' or 'against nature', *para phusin* in the Greek, is used positively later in Romans to describe God's action in saving the Gentiles, which is compared to grafting a wild olive tree 'against nature' into a cultivated tree (Rom. 11:24). As Eugene Rogers and Dale Martin have pointed out, this is not an act that violates nature but one that goes beyond what nature would have done alone.[53] Paul is sharing some of the assumptions of his day about same-sex intercourse, and with that we face a question: is it faithful *to the text itself* to use this reference (which he makes illustratively and in passing) to exclude a particular group of people from salvation, fellowship, or full participation in the Church, when the overarching argument of Romans is that God, in God's goodness, acted against nature to include, unexpectedly, those who had been outside the covenant?

Conclusion

We see, then, that there are many questions about each of these passages individually, questions that make it difficult to build a solid case against same-sex relationships from any one of them, or even from all of them taken together. What these verses meant in their original context is frequently difficult to establish, not least when it comes to determining what exactly was being condemned, and why. But even beyond that question, even if we come to the conclusion that the Biblical writers were proposing a general disapproval of same-sex intercourse, there is the question of what those discussions mean for us today, as we try to respond in our own time, in a way that is based on the message of the

Bible taken as a whole. We need to remember the story of how the Church discerned its response to slavery, for example, and ask whether even the most cogent 'biblical case' against same-sex relationships is ultimately like the 'biblical case' for slavery. Like the early abolitionists, we must be open to seeing that dedication to a particular understanding of some particular texts has prevented us from seeing broader truth which permeates the Bible as a whole.

So, we urge openness, but that openness is not openness to anything at all. It is an openness that works among the interrelated sources of Christian theology, morality, and practice, to discern what is good and what is not. We might frame that task in terms of the three-legged stool of Richard Hooker (1554-1600), with doctrine resting firmly because of the balance of Scripture, tradition, and reason. It might be described in terms of the 'Quadrilateral', sometimes associated with Methodism, of Scripture, tradition, reason, and experience. In either case, we find an established and broad agreement that Scripture and tradition are related to one another, that this involves reason, not least in the interpretation and application of what we've been given in Scripture and tradition, and that our experience – individually and corporately – plays a role.

Yes, there will continue to be some disagreement between more Protestant and more Catholic Christians about whether to stress an unmediated direct engagement with Scripture, or a reading of Scripture in the company of the historical voice of the tradition. Certainly, there will continue to be disagreement between more biblicist and more progressive traditions about how we should understand the relationship between Scripture and contemporary experience. However, those disagreements reside within a broader and shared agreement that the Bible is the foundation for our thinking, that Christians do not read the Bible in isolation from others, either now or in the past, and that reading involves reason. The Bible itself arose through a long, historical journey, both when its contents were being written and edited, and during the period when the limits of the canon – as an agreed, authoritative collection of books – was debated and agreed upon. It has been preserved, taught, interpreted, and debated within a long and diverse tradition of Christianity. In all of these ways, there has always been an evident interrelatedness between Scripture, tradition, reason, and experience.

One of the problems to date with debates between Christians who oppose same-sex relationships and those who support them is that many of the loudest voices in the debate have been arguing in a one-dimensional way. They have not reflected the breadth of what it is really like to be a Christian and discern together about how to live: reasoning, from Scripture, in dialogue with experience, in the company of the tradition. Thus, one party has talked about Scripture as if interpretation was not a demanding task, involving reason, necessarily carried out together, within the wisdom of a tradition that is bigger than any one of us, or as if we read the Bible in a vacuum, without bringing our experiences to bear (which we do, in fact, in any act of reading). But then, the other party has too often made experience its one source, and has too often treated Scripture as a problem, rather than as the Christian foundation. Similarly, it has often treated reason as almost synonymous with feelings, and fallen foul of what C. S. Lewis (1898-1963) called 'chronological snobbery' in its willingness to elevate itself above the tradition of Christian theology, philosophy and ethics.[54]

One party is adamant that the Bible clearly prohibits same-sex intercourse, whatever the setting might be, and that this must be the beginning and end of the conversation. The other party is adamant that since we now know what we do about human biology and psychology, alongside our experiences of contemporary life and culture, we should be inclusive of gay, lesbian, and bisexual people and relationships, as the beginning and end of the conversation. Is it any wonder we continue to talk past one another?

What would happen, we wonder, if we could step back from these attachments to one-dimensional accounts of what it means to think and live in a Christian way, and take a wider view of Christian discipleship, in the light of all of the gifts that God has given us? What would happen if we turned to the riches of Scripture alongside the wisdom (and failures) of Christian tradition, taking care in our ways of reasoning, in conversation with the experience of people in history and today, alongside what the sciences help to illuminate about those experiences? And what would happen if the question posed was not, 'same-sex relationships: right or wrong?' – which is a limiting, brittle question – but rather something like 'What is the significance and purpose of sexuality and marriage in Christianity? What does sexuality and marriage look like in the way of Jesus Christ?', with consideration of same-sex relationships as part of *that*?

We suggest that we would find a wealth of insight, that we would find something wise and rather beautiful. In that light, we could understand and advocate a Christian understanding of sexuality and marriage more robustly and faithfully. This would resonate across Protestant and Catholic outlooks, and across traditional and liberal divisions, even where certain differences of emphasis and priorities may still exist. We might find that returning, together, to the question of what kinds of relationships can and cannot fulfil this vision of Christian relatedness would yield very different results from those generated by our current single-source-in-isolation, single-question approaches.

Chapter Four

Being Part of the Story

In our conversations, debates and disagreements about sexuality, we can easily talk about 'tradition' as if it were something static: a set of beliefs and practices set in stone. Looked at that way, while the world is changing all around us, the Church and its traditions stay the same. If, however, we look at two thousand years of Christian doctrine and history, we can see this is clearly not the case. The Christian tradition is dynamic, not static, and it is dynamic for distinctive *theological* reasons.

As followers of Jesus, we believe that God took human form and participated in our world, with all its joys and sorrows, as Jesus of Nazareth. That's the key to our relationship with God. Ascended to the Father, Jesus sent the Holy Spirit into the world, to sustain our relationship with God. Our task, as Christian disciples, is to discern when, where, and how that happens.

This relates to the way we read Scripture, which we discussed in the previous chapter. Reading the Bible lies at the heart of the life of the Church, as its supremely *generative* activity. One reason that we find the Biblical texts so productive is that we can, and do, bring our whole selves to them. We each bring our questions to the Bible, and the Holy Spirit works in response to our questions and experience as we wrestle with Scripture: texts come alive when we bring our questions to them, and that is all the more true for the Bible, not less. We can understand Christian tradition, in part, as the readings of Scripture that each generation makes afresh, as we bring our lives to the text and the text to our lives. Out of this we form our patterns of Christian discipleship, and our theological understanding of the world.

In this chapter, we will look at three examples of how the Christian tradition has developed, sometimes quite dramatically. Each involves sexuality and marriage; each is a story about the task of understanding Scripture.

Marriage and celibacy

Our first example is marriage and celibacy. The earliest Christians – by which we mean those who lived in the first two or three centuries – grappled with the question of whether marriage or celibacy was the ideal way of life. We know that these early Christians particularly grappled with some specific biblical texts, including Matthew 19, Mark 10 and 1 Corinthians 7.

Some of them lived with a profound sense of Christ's imminent second coming, and were therefore inclined to think that relationships such as marriage were best avoided, in anticipation of the new age. Some groups, including the Montanists, especially in the hills of Asia Minor and Syria, chose to live in a profoundly ascetic way (and urged others to do the same), embracing celibacy as one important way for them to break their connection with a world that they saw as profoundly sinful.[55] Others, such as Clement of Alexandria (150 – 215), believed that both celibacy and marriage were equally valid callings, and that each calling had its own distinctive sense of service and ministry to God.[56] What was the right way forward? Was marriage to be the Christian norm – as it was in the wider pagan world of the Roman Empire? Or for Christians was celibacy the higher ideal to strive for? The early Churches thought hard about that.

A key biblical text in all of this was 1 Corinthians 7, especially verses 7 to 9, in which Paul writes:

> I wish that all were as I myself am. But each has a particular gift from God, one having one kind and another a different kind. To the unmarried and the widows I say that it is well for them to remain unmarried as I am. But if they are not practising self-control, they should marry. For it is better to marry than be aflame with passion.

Did Paul mean that the higher good, the ideal to which all should aspire, is celibacy? Is marriage therefore a second best, a last resort, if we can't control our lust? Or did he really mean that people have different gifts – of celibacy and marriage – and that these are equally valid? These questions of interpretation have been much debated in Christian history. By the fourth century the majority of scholarly Christians leaders were quite clear: celibacy was the higher good, and marriage was second best. Throughout the fourth and fifth centuries, theologians such as Gregory of Nyssa (c. 331–394) in the East and Ambrose (c. 340–397) in the West wrote works in favour of virginity and celibacy.[57] That would remain the Church's attitude throughout the following 1100 years, during which monastic life flourished, and celibacy came to be expected for clergy in the Western Church (and in the later Middle Ages, required). One consequence of this was that the clergy were held to a different standard of moral behaviour in the sexual realm than lay people. A particular interpretation of the first part of verse 7 of 1 Corinthians had won out. The emphasis was on Paul's statement, 'I wish that all were as I myself am.'

It was Martin Luther (1483–1546) in the sixteenth century who made a 180-degree turn on the interpretation of this text, and shattered the idea that the clergy should be set apart from the laity. This came with his emphasis on 'the priesthood of all believers'. If all stand equally before God, he asked, why couldn't priests marry? Why should we suppose that everyone called to priesthood is also called to celibacy? And if we can't, why should those who are called to priesthood, but not to celibacy, be forced to remain celibate? This is what he began to preach in the 1520s. That preaching, joined by the efforts of other reformers, brought about a sea change in the Church.

Luther made this extraordinary shift through a different approach to the Bible, and especially to 1 Corinthians 7. Instead of emphasising Paul's phrase 'I wish all were as I myself am' as an argument in favour of celibacy, Luther emphasised the idea that 'it is better to marry than to be aflame with passion'. He often quoted this in his sermons in conjunction with verse 2: 'because of sexual immorality, each man should have his own wife, and each woman her own husband.' From this, he argued in favour of marriage as a means of regulating sexual desire. [58]

He also put forward some positive arguments, especially the idea that human beings were not meant to be alone (Gen. 2:18), but should rather enjoy the companionship that marriage allowed, as well as writing positively about the virtues of marital sex. Since the Reformation, Luther's ideas have held sway within the Protestant Churches, and in Anglicanism: the idea that the majority will be called to marry, whilst only a very few will have the calling to celibacy. [59]

This first example illustrates the massive shifts that have occurred in Christian history as the Church and its theologians have grappled with Scripture in light of their own experiences and questions.

Birth control

Our second example illustrates the ways in which the Anglican Churches have responded *intentionally* to new situations in the world, in this case by deciding to change its teaching on contraception. By the early twentieth century, reliable birth control was being introduced, and attitudes to marriage and sexuality were changing quickly. World War I gave greater freedom to women and men, in England and elsewhere, since supplying chaperones was no longer practically possible for women and men of the upper and middle classes, and a new urgency was given to love and marriage amongst people of all classes in the face of war. This often resulted in speedy marriages, and children born out of wedlock, as young men were sent to the Front and to the possibility of an early death in battle. The new freedoms were not handed back when the war ended in 1918.

All the same, in 1920, the Lambeth Conference restated the Church's longstanding position prohibiting the use of artificial methods of contraception, in Resolution 68:

> The Conference... regards with grave concern the spread in modern society of theories and practices hostile to the modern family. We utter an emphatic warning against the use of unnatural means for the avoidance of conception, together with the grave dangers – physical, moral and religious – thereby

incurred and the evils with which the extension of such use threatens the human race. In opposition to the teaching which, under the name of science and religion, encourages married people in the deliberate cultivation of sexual union as an end in itself, we steadfastly uphold what must always be regarded as the governing considerations of Christian marriage. One is the primary purpose for which marriage exists, namely the continuation of the race through the gift and heritage of children; the other is the paramount importance in married life of deliberate and thoughtful self-control.[60]

The 1920s saw rapid changes. Open and frank discussions about both sex and birth control became more widespread. London's first birth control clinic was opened in 1921, where women could go for advice on contraception and be fitted with the cervical cap. Twenty thousand women visited the clinic in the first three months.

All of this had an effect on the bishops' thinking, as they themselves declared in Resolution 9 at the Lambeth Conference in 1930: 'The Conference believes that the conditions of modern life call for a fresh statement from the Christian Church on the subject of sex.' What the bishops now said about the use of contraception was markedly different from what they had said in their resolution of 1920. They declared that artificial forms of birth control were permissible for married couples in certain circumstances (Resolution 15):

> Where there is a clearly felt moral obligation to limit or avoid parenthood, the method must be decided on Christian principles. The primary and obvious method is complete abstinence from intercourse (as far as may be necessary) in a life of discipline and self-control lived in the power of the Holy Spirit. Nevertheless in those cases where there is such a clearly-felt moral obligation to limit or avoid parenthood, and where there is a morally sound reason for avoiding complete abstinence, the Conference agrees that other methods may be used, provided that this is done in the light of the same Christian principles. The conference records its strong condemnation of the use of any methods of conception control from motives of luxury, selfishness, or mere convenience.

This was a tentative seal of approval for contraception, even though Lambeth resolutions were not (and are still not) binding on any individual Anglican province. All the same, the bishops' 1930 statement represented a significant shift in thinking. The bishops knew that they were going against a long-standing Christian tradition: 'We acknowledge the weight of that testimony, but we are unable to accept that tradition as final.' In making that shift, they took account of 'a full appreciation of facts and conditions which were not present in the past, but which are due to modern civilization.' They also took note of people's lived experiences: 'there are circumstances in married life which justify, and even demand, the limitation of the family by *some* means.' There were, they said, 'moral situations which may make it obligatory to use other methods.'[61] Almost ninety years on, this is even more generally accepted.[62]

Sexual difference and complementarity

Our final example concerns a topic we have already touched on: our ideas about differences between the sexes, and their relation. Crucially, the way in which this has been understood also turns out to be an evolving story.

Before the modern period, scientists – still relying on ancient sources such as Galen – understood woman as an imperfect version of man. They believed that there was 'one sex', hierarchically arranged. Women and men were seen as having the same sexual organs; it was just that women's were on the interior.[63] We are not talking about two different but equal ways of being human, but about a single way of being human that either succeeded (men) or at least partially failed (women).[64]

This 'one-sex' idea was challenged in the eighteenth century, in the Enlightenment: it was challenged by science, but by science driven by political change. The old hierarchies were being questioned, as revolutions occurred in both France and America. Universal rights were championed, but uneasily: was everyone really equal? The answer was sought in the supposed 'facts' of biology. The search for anatomical sexual differences in this period was driven by an increased sense that women were intrinsically different from men – and, on those grounds, should not receive the same rights. The result was the articulation of two sexes.

As we have already seen, sexual difference – or the notion of two sexes presented in this way – is rather less clear-cut than we might imagine, as medical cases of those who find themselves biologically between the sexes illustrate. But the important point is that sexual difference was imbued with political ideology from the beginning. Out of all this came the notion of the *complementarity* of the sexes: the idea that women and men have distinctly different qualities (rooted in biology), and that this suits them for different (but 'complementary') roles in life. This sort of distinction went down well in the economic climate of the newly industrialised West. As work became separated from home, newly defined middle and working classes emerged. Separate spheres for work and home developed, and home came to be seen as the special domain of women – at least, of middle-class women – whose 'natural' characteristics of gentleness and passivity made them keepers of morals and preservers of the hearth.

Many preachers took on gender complementarity with enthusiasm. New ideas about the differences between men and women were given a theological spin, and blended with old ideas about the subordination of women. Women were seen as spiritually equal, but, in practical terms, socially subordinate. These ideas were taken around the world by missionaries and servants of the Empire alike, and imposed on cultures with previously completely different cultural arrangements of the sexes and relations of kinship.[65]

These ideas did not go uncontested. In the nineteenth century, women argued for their admission to higher education, for universal suffrage, and for married women to be able to own property. All the same, those newly established ideas of sexual difference, those surprisingly recent approaches to complementarity, continued to have a powerful impact on theology, most notably in the work of Karl Barth (1886–1968), who insisted that the 'distinctive natures' of men and women were 'the command of God'.[66] For Barth, these distinctive natures led to sex-differentiated functions, which were absolutely rigid: 'The sexes might wish to exchange their special vocations, what is required of the one or the other as such. This must not happen.'[67] As a consequence – and this is a real problem – we see concepts of sexual difference and complementarity that our ancestors would barely have recognised 300 years ago, let alone 3000 years ago, read back on to the

Hebrew Scriptures, especially the creation stories in Genesis 2.

These three examples – marriage and celibacy, birth control, and gender complementarity – have barely touched on questions of homosexuality. With them, we have taken a step back, to give examples of ways in which the Christian tradition has changed and shifted in response to its own readings of Scripture, in response to a changing culture, and in response to new ideas in science.[68] None of this should surprise us, for it is of the very nature of Christian tradition to be dynamic, not static; the vocation of all Christians is to discern the continuing work of God, through the Holy Spirit, which blows where it will (John 3:8). It is to that theological picture that we now turn.

A theological story

God's revelation unfolds. It takes time. The unfolding story told by the Bible itself gives us plenty of examples of that. A good one concerns teaching about retribution – 'an eye for an eye' – in Exodus 21:23-5 (and also in Lev. 24:20 and Deut. 19:21), and then from Jesus (in Matt. 5:38-42).

We might find the phrase 'an eye for an eye' harsh, but it is a radical development in justice, if it is taken against a backdrop of unrestrained vengeance. 'An eye for an eye' calls its hearers to fairness and proportion:

the punishment must fit the crime, and not go beyond it. We see this all more clearly if we look at the whole passage in Exodus: 'If any harm follows, then you shall give life for life, eye for eye, tooth for tooth, hand for hand, foot for foot, burn for burn, wound for wound, stripe for stripe' (Exodus 21:23-5). It is all about proportion.

Surprising as it might look to some, then, 'an eye for an eye' represents a great leap forward in the ethical history of humanity.[69] All the same, Jesus did not leave it there, and he taught a yet more glorious (and difficult) principle, of forgiveness:

> You have heard that it was said, 'An eye for an eye and a tooth for a tooth.' But I say to you, Do not resist an evildoer. But if anyone strikes you on the right cheek, turn the other also; and if anyone wants to sue you and take your coat, give your cloak as well; and if anyone forces you to go one mile, go also the second mile. Give to everyone who begs from you, and do not refuse anyone who wants to borrow from you (Matt. 5:38-42).

The words of the law limited disproportionate fury in response to wrongdoing. Jesus proposed an even more perfect way to live, where forgiveness and mercy overcome the desire for harm in return for harm. This is tremendously important, for instance, when it comes to putting an end to cycles of violence.

Jesus moved things on. Is Exodus therefore faulty?
Or Leviticus, or Deuteronomy? No. They are not faulty;
they are simply not the last word on the topic. God
teaches us, and that teaching takes time, whether God is
teaching an individual, or the whole human race. Jesus
himself made it clear that the process of discerning the
will of God, the process of discerning what is right and
good, of learning the truth about God, would take time,
that it would continue, indeed, beyond his Ascension:

> I still have many things to say to you, but you
> cannot bear them now. When the Spirit of truth
> comes, he will guide you into all the truth; for he
> will not speak on his own, but will speak whatever
> he hears, and he will declare to you the things that
> are to come (John 16:12-13).

An important way to describe what it means for the
Bible to be true in this dynamic way, and a way to see
why that is so, comes from John Calvin (1509-64).
Good communication, he appreciated, speaks to its
audience in a way that the audience can understand. It
'communicates' to them. In God's revelation to us, God
speaks in a way that we can assimilate. Calvin called this
God's 'accommodation' to our state:

> who is so devoid of intellect as not to understand
> that God... lisps with us as nurses are wont to do
> with little children? Such modes of expression...

accommodate the knowledge of him to our feebleness. In doing so, he must, of course, stoop far below his proper height.[70]

That is how we might understand Genesis 1-2, for instance, to be manifestly true, without supposing that it stands in conflict with what modern science teaches us about the age of the universe, or the evolution of life, or the nature of men and women. God accommodates divine truth to human communication, using forms and figures that speak to us (such as poetry, in Genesis 1, for instance). God spoke through the author of Genesis what the readers of Genesis could understand.

Revelation unfolds in time, and after revelation is complete, the task of unfolding the meaning of revelation then becomes central to the life of the Church. In theological matters, that task is often called the 'development of doctrine'. Thinking about God, for instance, has taught us that God is three Persons in one Nature. Or, of Christ we say that he is one Person, both human and divine. Neither of those ideas is laid out in just that form in the Bible, but both are a faithful account of what God teaches in the Bible, taken as a whole, and thought through prayerfully by centuries of Christians.

The principle of development also applies in moral matters. Slavery – which we have already mentioned in this book a number of times – is the most obvious example. The rejection of slavery emerged from the careful, unfolding work of paying attention to Scripture as a whole, of thinking about it reasonably, and in relation to experience of human life. We do not find such a prohibition in any one place in the Bible: quite the opposite. But considered reflection on the Bible on the whole gave us that prohibition.

An important part of the task of developing the theological and moral mind of the Church is to discern where the revolutionary message of the Bible lies, and what simply reflects the common assumptions of the time. As an example, consider these comments in Ephesians about husbands and wives:

> Wives, be subject to your husbands as you are to the Lord. For the husband is the head of the wife just as Christ is the head of the Church. Just as the Church is subject to Christ, so also wives ought to be, in everything, to their husbands. Husbands, love your wives, just as Christ loved the Church and gave himself up for her, in order to make her holy (Eph. 5:22-26).

The first comment was nothing new: 'Wives, be subject to your husbands'. It represents the common assumptions of the first century. The second phrase *is* startling, however, and new: 'Husbands, love your wives, just as Christ loved the Church and gave himself up for her'. Too often, when Christians have thought about the relationships between a husband and wife in marriage, and invoked this passage, they have been fixated by what reflects the culture of the time, and perhaps simply passed it on, and they have ignored the moral thunderclap: 'Husbands, love your wives, just as Christ loved the Church'.

Today, a good many Christians believe that the message of human dignity and equality, found elsewhere in the Bible,[71] shows that the assumption of an unequal relationship between men and women in marriage found in this passage in Ephesians (wives are obedient, while husbands are not; the love of a husband reflects Christ's love, not the love of a wife) is not the point we should suppose that revelation is making. Christians can have a vision of marriage marked by equality, and – rightly – they hold that they have theological reasons for thinking that way. The passage from Ephesians is not set aside; it is interpreted by, and feeds into, a wider picture.

We think that the same principle applies to discernments about same-sex relationships. The Scriptures teach a vision of life and love that is truly revolutionary. We learn, for instance, that we are most truly ourselves when we live for others, and that we gain life not by clutching to it, but by giving it away. We learn that this living-for-others underlies the truest meaning of sexuality. Christians have discerned that most people flourish best when this living-for-others finds its focus in commitment to one other person: when a couple make a life-long commitment, within which sex most properly belongs. *That* is the revolutionary message when it comes to sexual ethics, and not the ways in which the Bible reflects assumptions about sex between two men or two women. We say that, not least, because sex between two men or two women within a monogamous, life-long commitment was not something the Biblical authors were ever writing about.

The unfolding message of revelation, and the ongoing process of discerning the meaning of revelation as a whole, need not stand in conflict with the best of what either modern science, or our own direct observation, shows us about the possibilities for committed same-sex love. That isn't about selling out the Church's teaching to prevailing cultural assumptions. Rather, it opens up the possibility that we might commend God's often profoundly counter-cultural message about the truest meaning of sexual love to *everyone*.

Chapter Five

Being in Love

Most of this short book explains why we think it's good for Christians to embrace their gay and lesbian brothers and sisters, and to celebrate their relationships. That's no abstract matter: it's about how we treat and relate to people who worship in our churches; it's about people on your street, with whom you want to discuss your faith; it's about many readers of this book. Sexual intercourse is part of these relationships, although not the only part. We think that the Church should be willing – delighted even – to hallow and strengthen such commitments.

Up to now, this book has tackled prohibitions and assumptions against same-sex relationships. As part of that, we have thought about how Christians develop their sense of right and wrong. We have thought about the Bible, recognising that it needs to be approached as a whole, as God's unfolding revelation. We have considered lessons from history, wanting to place our current thinking in the great sweep of Christian thought. We have been reminded that what we take for granted today hasn't always been seen like that. We have turned to science, and what it teaches us about the world, since we can't work out what to say about anything until we know what that something *is* as best we can.

We've explained why we think Christians can change their minds, positively, about sexual relationships between two men or two women. Although rejection of such relationships is often presented as if it were the touchstone of orthodoxy, it's perfectly possible to see endorsing gay and lesbian relationships as being in complete concord with the rest of the faith. Changing our minds about same-sex relationships *isn't* about changing our minds about Christianity: treating lesbian and gay people generously actually fits better with the broad mind of the Church. Many of us writing this book have been on that journey.

All of that – this book so far – has been about clearing the ground for acting and relating differently. It gives permission. Faithfulness to the Bible, and a passion for the truth – truth shown by theology, and truth shown by science, each in its way – sits comfortably with the kind of cheerful acceptances of same-sex relationships that most people today find comes naturally.

The ground is open for a move on that front, if we want to make that move. But, to do that, do we first also need some special theology of same-sex love?

No – we don't. Love is love.

Same-sex relationships can be good (and very often are, although everyone falls short of perfection) for the same reasons that opposite-sex relationship can be good (with the same comments about human frailty).

The reasons for supporting them are therefore the same. We can rejoice in love between two women, or two men, simply because it's love. We can take this love – these relationships, these people – into the heart of the Church because that's what we do with love, with relationships, and with people.

When two men, or two women, want to commit themselves to a life lived together, through thick and thin, the reasons for blessing them (and for blessing that promise) are the reasons why we'd bless anyone: because we are thankful for them, and their commitment, because a blessing recognises a vocation, because we see that this relationship makes for life and abundance of life, because we know our frailty and we want God's protection for it, and because there is a commitment in front of us that points to what God's coming kingdom is all about.[72] Nor would we be celebrating such a relationship in isolation: any mature Christian relationship looks beyond itself, seeking to enrich society and strengthen the community.[73]

We can move on when it comes to same-sex love, as individual Christians, and as a Church. It doesn't call for some 'new theology' for gay people. It does call for bravery.

The reason for acting bravely is simply that love is love, and because love is a reflection of God in the world: a reflection shown in joy and faithfulness, through trial and sorrow, in lives – like God's own Trinitarian life – lived beyond themselves, for the sake of another.

Chapter Six

Being Missional

This final chapter examines how attitudes to same-sex relationships impact on the Church's ability to communicate the gospel today. In some ways this is the most important question of all. As long ago as 1931 Emil Brunner (1889-1966) observed that:

> Mission work does not arise from any arrogance in the Christian Church; mission is its cause and its life. The Church exists by mission, just as a fire exists by burning. Where there is no mission, there is no Church; and where there is neither Church nor mission, there is no faith.[74]

Mission is both a practical matter and a theological one, and both aspects need to be remembered as we think about same-sex relationships.

Here is the wider picture: the Church of England has been experiencing catastrophic numerical decline. Its membership is ageing significantly, too. In England today, an 81 year old is 8 times more likely to be part of a church than an 18 year old. That points to further numerical decline just round the corner. A generation is growing up who have never known the Church as part of their lives. It matters that they are not connecting with the Church as young people because, historically, that is when the link is made: research indicates that 84% of Christians came to faith before they were 25, but only 1% after 45.

This calls for action. We cannot put our heads in the sand. Thankfully, many Anglicans are looking for new paths in mission. The term 'evangelism' has not, historically, had universal appeal, but today things have changed. The 2015-20 General Synod is giving serious attention to the Church's membership crisis, and a new strategy for renewal and reform is emerging. In his Presidential Address to the General Synod on 16 February 2016, Archbishop Justin Welby said that

> For too long the ministry of evangelism in the Church has been viewed as an app on the system … apps are simply add-ons, optional extras, suited to those with particular interests and activities. As I said, for many it seems that evangelism is such an app – simply to be used for those who are gifted, who don't mind being out of their comfort zones, who are happy talking about faith with strangers, and have a clever way of explaining the mysteries of God's love. But evangelism and witness are not an app. They are the operating system itself.

The challenge is to embrace genuine missional change, not merely rearranging the deckchairs on the *Titanic*.

To deliver this, the Church needs to look outwards and engage deeply with the realities of the lives of those it is seeking to reach for Christ.

We need to be real about who they are, and what matters for them. C. S. Lewis once observed that 'The proper study of shepherds is sheep, not (save accidentally) other shepherds. And woe to you if you do not evangelise.'[75] We not only have to understand what matters for people outside the church, but also how they perceive it. If all they hear is judgment, rather than love, they will not come to Christ. Yes, there is a call to repentance in the gospel, but that must not hide the fact that Christ was sent into the world not to condemn it, but that through him the world might be saved (John 3:17). Evangelism means loving people, as God loves them.

This timeless glorious vision can only be delivered if we are honest about the realities we face. Contemporary culture poses major challenges, but it also offers real opportunities, if we have the courage and faith to grasp them. Most people are turned off by institutional religion. They no longer see it as a place that reflects their values and best aspirations. That said, many are longing for real love and community, and are even haunted by the possibility of God in their lives. A recent survey of people who claim 'No religion' reveals that only 10% of them are actively secularist. 90% have broader spiritual imagination and yearnings.

Most disturbingly, however, many people are beginning to see the Church as not just an irrelevance, but as a toxic brand. This happens especially when it is perceived as being weak on equality and human rights: on justice and human dignity. The Church needs to take seriously the fact that people's commitment to these standards is a moral and ethical imperative, not some secularist whimsy.

In fact, the UN Declaration of Human Rights has profoundly Christian roots. Its framers saw the twentieth century's wars as failures of Christendom. They therefore tried to articulate a Christian moral vision afresh, engaging everybody, not just Church members.[76] They have succeeded: human rights have become core public values.

Closer to home, the UK Equality Act 2010 offers legal protection against discrimination based on age, disability, gender reassignment, marriage, pregnancy and maternity, race, religion and belief, sex and sexual orientation. Most people are utterly bewildered when they see a Church that seems not to share these values and is unprepared to hold itself accountable to them.

Equality and diversity are now normative virtues in almost all public contexts, except the Church. Getting its house in order about them will not necessarily attract new members, but it may help stem the drain. People who find the way the Church treats gay and lesbian people unfair and immoral would find it easier to stay in a more inclusive Church.

To renew our commitment to mission means returning to the Church's primary duty: to 'bring the grace and truth of Christ to this particular generation, and make him known to those within our care', that the world may believe.[77] Addressing the Church's reputation for excluding, even victimizing, non-heterosexual people is not just a matter of window dressing. First of all, it is what justice demands, and then – because the people we want to reach recognise that – it is also what faithfulness in mission requires.

The prophetic agenda of the Kingdom is to 'do justice, love mercy, and walk humbly with our God' (Micah 6:8). The point we've made in this book is that justice, mercy and humility urge us to welcome gay and lesbian people, and their love and relationships.

The Church's job is to be good news in its context. Justice is the public face of love. Jesus sent out disciples in pairs not to sell something under pressure, but to receive hospitality: to live with people and be good news among them. Paul's mission did not impose alien values from afar. He became all things to all people that by any means possible he might save some, for the sake of the Gospel (1 Cor. 9:22-23). This is how Christianity spread in all cultures, taking everyone seriously as the people they were, authentically communicating the all-embracing love of Jesus. Paul did not set himself over and against the best moral instincts of his hearers. He described evangelism as 'commending good news to the common conscience of all' (2 Cor. 4:2). Paying attention to particularities of the people the Church serves is a key missionary discipline.

To enable the Church to do this today, there is useful data about its key missing demographic, young adults under 35. In 2007, the Archbishops' Council commissioned the *Weddings Project* to understand how young adults getting married in church and elsewhere saw the Church. Findings were surprisingly positive. As many as 75% of young adults saw the church as the best place to celebrate the most significant commitment of their life to another person. Sadly, many disqualified themselves, fearing a lack of welcome or understanding. Those who made it through the door, however, experienced something overwhelmingly positive.

Those who had married in Church were asked why their experience had been so engaging and positive, when it had been. The answer came back loud and clear: it mattered that the service had been personal, special (some even said 'holy'), and authentic.

It was heartening to learn that, contrary to expectation perhaps, marriage and relationships do matter very much to young adults. We also know that they are completely baffled that gay and lesbian people should be excluded from this way of life.[78] A 2016 YouGov poll indicates that 93% of the Church's key lost demographic, unaffiliated 25-35's, believe same-sex marriage is right. Unless there is a really good reason for opposing same-sex relationships – and we don't believe that there is – we are shooting ourselves in the foot in the worst possible way.

This is apparent from the experience of serving college chaplains with responsibility for student welfare:

> The collar makes me a symbol of views on sexuality that most students can't fathom, and would never condone. I make a point of distancing myself from the Church's pronouncements on the same-sex question. I couldn't do my job otherwise.[79]

> I am glad to offer a spiritual home to the Christian who has been told they are not welcome at communion at their former church, and at the same time to be an expression of a loving Christianity which listens hard to, and takes seriously, those whose clearly delineated faiths mean that they struggle to accept their non-heterosexual brothers and sisters in the possibility of their flourishing relationships.[80]

> The reaction of many students to the Church's current pronouncements on gay marriage and the more general issue of homosexual relationships is one that veers between complete bafflement and catatonic indifference... their attitude is one not only of acceptance, but of commitment to the cause of many people in the world who are marginalised and persecuted for their sexuality.[81]

Having worked closely with teenagers in schools and colleges over the past 15 years my general assessment of their ethical stance is that it is resoundingly evidence-based and this-worldly (and this goes even for the religious ones!). At heart, morality for the young is a simple science: sin results in damage and hurt, agape in happiness and joy. Given such an approach the sexual pronouncements of ancient texts find it very hard even to muster an audience.[82]

For students, living in a society where someone's sexuality is a personal, not a legal, matter, the position of the Church of England is a cause of bewilderment. Our teaching on sex and sexuality, about consent, the importance of stability and commitment in relationships, and on marriage, is often well received in debate and discussion. But then comes the 'gay thing' – that somehow our wholesome teaching doesn't apply if you're gay – and our affirmations look shallow, about as affirming as welcoming the left-handed so long as they don't use their left hand. Students see through this; they are bewildered, even amused, at our moral and linguistic gymnastics.[83]

A Church committed to mission in the real world has to ask 'How on earth can we reach out to them?' And actively reach out it must. During most of the previous

1600 years, Christianity has been taken for granted. It's been part and parcel of the order of things: the royal arms in many of our ancient churches illustrate that. But now Christianity no longer has this privileged position. Christians have to convince others by the lives they lead, not the power they wield. The Church is having to resume its original character as a movement or pilgrimage. The way its message resonates with the moral instincts of people today is more important than ever.

Relationships, and the ways people are treated, are the heart of mission. Jesus said: 'By this everyone will know that you are my disciples, if you have love for one another' (John 13:35). Christianity is not an ideology, but a way of life that is contagious when it is lived authentically. Its principal invitation is to 'taste and see that the Lord is good' (Psalm 34:8). If people taste and see, and it seems that the Lord is not so good for the person they are, or for people they love, that is disastrous.

We have to admit it: the Church's inherited moral disapproval of gay people is known to have caused much cruelty and misery. A great many have suffered, and that puts a lot of people off today, not just those who have been affected most directly.

This disapproval has often had gruesome consequences: there have even been suicides, as we mentioned in the first chapter. We can be sure that the Church did not learn this from Christ. The fruit of the

Spirit is love, joy, peace, self-control, justice and hope, not shame, self-loathing, and helplessness.

This message is especially important in a world of bad news, gripped by a growing fear of extremist terrorism. People do know that much violence is politically and tribally driven, but frighteningly often they hear people claim the right to do terrible deeds in the name of their religion. Daesh (or 'ISIS') videos show people committing barbaric acts 'for God', among them, the oppression of women and the execution of gay people. A Church that is seen to deny equality to gay people will have to work increasingly hard to distance itself from fundamentalist extremism in the public imagination.

In fact, it has become well-nigh impossible to articulate a theological conviction that loving and faithful gay relationships are wrong without seeming extreme and fundamentalist. Most people just cannot see how excluding certain people because of who they are, and who they love, can possibly contribute to the common good.

It doesn't, and we don't have to exclude them. History, careful study of Scripture, and a grasp of the realities uncovered by science allow us to treat being gay not as unnatural or anomalous, but simply as a variant within the human condition.

What possibilities does this shift open up for the Church? Some gay Christians have been hanging on by their fingernails, not recognising what is glibly said about them, but continuing to love and pray for change.

Many are tired. Some have given up and left, reluctantly and painfully. Some of those people continue in faith, while others have been so damaged that they can no longer believe. Along with their heterosexual friends and families, many give the Church a wide berth because they feel its moral standards are lower than their own. They cannot imagine how anyone can still be hung up about gay people, or see them as a problem.

Time heals. Future Christians won't see things as their grandparents did. Already younger Christians seem to have almost no energy for bickering about gays. They are seen as naturally equal to everyone else. Marriage is a way of life founded on love and faithfulness, so why not for all? Latest figures indicate that only 23% of Anglican men and 14% of Anglican women under 35 object to same-sex marriage. Tellingly, by far the largest segment of Anglicans who find it difficult to believe that gay people's relationships could be called marriage are men over 55. At present they hold most of the power, but this will not be the case for ever.

Time does indeed heal, but missional reality is too urgent to allow the Church to wait for time to solve this issue. Dragging our feet is neither sensible, nor ethical. As long as we prevaricate about gay relationships, and continue to wring our hands, gay people remain excluded (and any platitudes we might add about affirming them all the same remain just that – platitudes). The litmus test is that they cannot celebrate holy relationships in church. Good ordinands are forced to choose between their vocations and loving, faithful relationships. Some try to combine the two, but feel the strain. Others deny feelings of love for the sake of Church teaching, and are diminished as a result. Some people with great gifts, who want to serve the Church full-time, find they can't do it and deny who they are, or turn their backs on someone they love. Either way, they lose out, and so does the Church.

The reality is urgent. It might be more comfortable for many to support the status quo, or remain in indecision, when in fact they know which way this ought to go, but gay and lesbian people continue to pay the price for that, and a generation is being lost to faith in Christ.

This is not just about loving our gay neighbours as ourselves. The Church's present paralysis is actively wrecking the faith of some of its most committed straight members. Here is a recent letter to a bishop:

> I attend a local church and am on the PCC and a former Deputy Church Warden. I don't profess to be a great theologian — just an ordinary man — but I do consider myself to be a Christian and 'love thy neighbour' is at the heart of everything I believe. I am 48, happily married, one son, but do have gay friends and family and I don't view them as sinners who need to be put to death...

Our Vicar... posted on the church website that 'we' were proud to support Anglican Mainstream... Obviously this was not the view of the PCC [and] after much begrudging passive resistance, it was changed...

Yesterday our reading was Romans 1:18-32 and then a sermon about this with references to 'the sin of equality' and references to 'inter sex morality' (whatever that is). I felt that the Sermon was slippery in that it was a full frontal assault on people that happen to be gay and lumping them as depraved, wicked, evil, murderers full of strife and deceit and that they deserve death, but cleverly hidden behind lawyer-type speak that stopped one step short of a) being criminal and b) clearly stepping over the line in terms that the congregation would actually understand.

I was so troubled by this that I could not bring myself to reply 'Thanks be to God' nor could I bring myself to take Communion. I find it deeply troubling that in the twenty-first century this clearly homophobic behaviour can be allowed to be practiced...

I am not doubting my own faith, but am just not quite knowing what to do. Trying to have a different point [of view] to our Vicar is a waste of time, as is trying to negotiate a compromise where he can maintain his beliefs without offending the rest of us. I feel like walking away, but not sure why I should and then I would be letting down others ...

I guess my question has no answer; but here goes: How can a simple layman like me prevent this type of extreme prejudice (and possibly criminal offence) from happening again. Should one just walk away and find a church, or Vicar, who is, quite frankly, more Christian?

This probably reads very badly, but it was cathartic at least in writing, so for that I thank you.

In a few years, there are likely to be hundreds of thousands of people in Britain living in same-sex households, and some of them, please God, will be Christians. This is a reality in the communities we serve. It's something that we all have to have a response to. We hope that pastors and parishes who want to reach out to these people will be given that opportunity.

There's a good precedent. Over many years the Church has managed to live with different points of view about the remarriage of divorced people. Some thought it wrong, others impossible, and they had theological grounds for saying so, but they did not force their theology on people who, equally sincerely, believed that God's grace was sufficient to mend the past and offer divorcees a fresh chance in marriage. Both positions existed alongside each other with integrity.

Flexibility here is all about what we take to be the basics of the faith, those matters about which we really ought to agree. From the beginning, the Church's core boundaries have been baptism and the creeds. In 1946, Archbishop Geoffrey Fisher (1887-1972) said of the Church of England

> We have no doctrine of our own – we only possess the Catholic doctrine of the Catholic Church enshrined in the Catholic creeds and those creeds we hold without addition or diminution.[84]

This is no time to elevate a hard line against gay marriage, or even against gay relationships, to the status of the creeds. Indeed, to do so in our present missional circumstances would be suicidal.

In every age Christians have struggled to believe that God's grace really is wide enough to embrace other Christians with whom they disagree. Every generation has to rediscover for itself that Jesus really did come for all, and that his body needs to value and embrace everyone for whom he died. The Church of England has to find a way to fulfill this gospel imperative today if it is to survive and flourish in the future.

Suggestions for Further Reading

Jacques Balthazart, *The Biology of Homosexuality* (New York: Oxford University Press, 2011). A standard work of reference on the biological bases for sexual orientation.

John Bradbury and Susannah Cornwall (eds), *Thinking Again about Marriage* (London: SCM Press, 2016). Aims to guide readers into the practice of thinking theologically about marriage generally.

Susannah Cornwall, *SCM Core Text: Theology and Sexuality* (London: SCM Press, 2013). Gives an overview of the theological debate surrounding sexuality.

Susannah Cornwall, *Sexuality: The Inclusive Church Resource* (London: Darton, Longman and Todd, 2014). Includes several personal stories as well as a major essay surveying the state of theological research on sexuality.

Nicholas Coulton (ed.), *The Bible, the Church and Homosexuality* (London: Darton, Longman & Todd, 2005). A short collection of essays.

Andrew Davison, *Why Sacraments?* (London: SPCK, 2013). Sets a discussion of same-sex marriage in the context of a broader discussion of the nature of marriage.

Andrew Davison, *Blessing*, (London: Canterbury Press, 2014). Explores what we are doing, theologically, when we bless people and undertakings such a marriage.

Duncan Dormor and Jeremy Morris (eds), *An Acceptable Sacrifice?: Homosexuality and the Church* (London: SPCK, 2007). A collection written from an English Anglican perspective.

Margaret Farley, *Just Love: A Framework for Christian Ethics* (London: Continuum, 2008). An important recent study of the moral characteristics of good sexual relationships.

David P. Gushee, *Changing Our Mind* (Canton, MI: David Crumm Media, second edition, 2015). A leading US evangelical ethicist talks about the value of same-sex relationships in a book that is frank about his own change of mind.

Jo Ind, *Memories of Bliss: God, Sex, and Us* (London: SCM Press, 2010). A personal theological reflection on how to 'live our sexualities well'.

Jeffrey John, *'Permanent, Faithful, Stable'* (London: Darton, Longman and Todd, revised edition, 2012). A short book that is already a classic.

Gareth Moore OP, *A Question of Truth: Christianity and Homosexuality* (London: Continuum, 2003). A frank discussion of the topic from a scholarly Roman Catholic perspective.

Eugene Rogers, *Sexuality and the Christian Body: Their Way into the Triune God* (Oxford: Blackwell, 1999). A demanding but rewarding treatment, which places sexuality within the context of a communitarian theology, drawing particularly on Karl Barth and Thomas Aquinas.

Eugene Rogers, *Theology and Sexuality: Classic and Contemporary Reading* (Oxford: Blackwell, 2002). An excellent single-volume collection of writing on this subject; it includes the text of Rowan Williams' important lecture, 'The Body's Grace'.

Jack Rogers, *Jesus, the Bible and Homosexuality* (Louisville, KY: Westminster John Knox Press, revised edition, 2009). Rogers, a former Moderator of the Presbyterian Church of the USA, talks about his own change of mind, and places the question in the context of the flourishing of the whole Church.

Adrian Thatcher, *Making Sense of Sex* (London: SPCK, 2012). A short theological survey of the meaning of sex and sexuality, from a leading writer in the field.

Matthew Vines, *God and the Gay Christian: The Biblical Case in Support of Same-Sex Relationships* (New York: Convergent Books, 2014). A gay Christian's account of what the Bible means for those seeking to live faithfully within a scriptural vision of life.

Alan Wilson, *More Perfect Union? Understanding Same-sex Marriage* (London: Darton, Longman and Todd, 2014). A recent book written out of many conversations with same-sex couples, as well as reflection on the Bible and the Christian tradition.

Notes

1 Bible references are taken given from the New Revised Standard Version Anglicized Edition, copyright 1989, 1995, Division of Christian Education of the National Council of the Churches of Christ in the United States of America. Used by permission. All rights reserved.

2 This book addresses same-sex relationships generally, rather than the question of same-sex marriage more specifically.

3 Just as the Church is currently thinking theologically about same-sex relationships, there is also a discussion to be had about how to welcome, listen to, and respond to people whose testimony to us is that their own sense of their gender does not correspond to the biological gender of their birth. This is a distinct question from discussions of same-sex relationships, and this is not the book to do it justice.

4 'Vicky Beeching, Christian rock star "I'm gay. God loves me just the way I am"', *The Independent*, 13 August 2014.

5 This particular tragedy was discussed in *Christianity Today* in December 2014: www.christiantoday.com/article/lizzie. lowe.suicide.what.help.can.churches.offer.teens.struggling. with.sexual.identity/44595.htm.

6 A significant number of distinguished contemporary theologians, deeply rooted in the heart of the Christian tradition, take an affirmative view of love between gay people. A small selection would include Eugene Rogers, author of *Thomas Aquinas and Karl Barth: Sacred Doctrine and the Natural Knowledge of God* (Notre Dame, IN: University of Notre Dame Press, 1995) and *The Holy Spirit: Classic and Contemporary Readings* (Chichester: Wiley-Blackwell, 2009),

and also of *Sexuality and the Christian Body: Their Way Into the Triune God* (Oxford: Blackwell, 1999); Graham Ward, author of *True Religion* (Oxford: Blackwell, 2002) and *The Politics of Discipleship* (Grand Rapids, Michigan: Baker Academic, 2009), and Catherine Pickstock, author of *AfterWriting: On the Liturgical Consummation of Philosophy,* (Oxford: Blackwell, 1997) and *Truth in Aquinas,* with John Milbank (London: Routledge 2001), who both contributed essays to *Queer Theology: Rethinking the Western Body* (ed. Gerard Loughlin, Blackwell 2007); James Allison, author of *Raising Abel: The Recovery of the Eschatological Imagination* (New York: Crossroad, 1996), and also of *Faith Beyond Resentment: Fragments Catholic and Gay* (London: DLT, 2001); Mark Jordan, author of *Rewritten Theology: Aquinas After His Readers* (2005, Chichester: Wiley-Blackwell), as well as *The Invention of Sodomy in Christian Theology* (Chicago: University of Chicago Press, 1997) and *Blessing Same-Sex Unions: The Perils of Queer Romance and the Confusions of Christian Marriage* (Chicago: University of Chicago Press, 2005), and Sarah Coakley, author of *Sacrifice Regained: Reconsidering the Rationality of Religious Belief* (Cambridge: Cambridge University Press, 2012), and also *God, Sexuality and the Self: An Essay 'On the Trinity'* (Cambridge: Cambridge University Press, 2013). Other theologians at the forefront of the current return to patristic theological sources, which could be described as a 'turn to orthodoxy' in Christian doctrinal and philosophical theology, take a strongly supportive position on same-sex relationships, on theological grounds.

7   Eugene Rogers, in particular, has argued forcefully in favour of the recognition of same-sex relationships by the Church (including their recognition as marriage) on the basis that committed, life-long, monogamous relationships are, for most people, their principal arena for spiritual discipline and sanctification. See 'Same-sex complementarity: A Theology of Marriage', May 11 2011, *The Christian Century*, 26-31, 'Marriage as an Ascetic Practice', *INTAMS Review, The Journal of the International Academy of Marital Spirituality*, 11 (2005), 28–

36, and Mark Jordan (ed.), *Authorizing Marriage: Canon, Tradition, and Critique in the Blessing of Same-Sex Unions* (Princeton, NJ: Princeton University Press, 2006).

8   Craig Hovey wrote about this in 'Christian Ethics as Good News' in Andrew Davison (ed.), *Imaginative Apologetics* (London: SCM Press, 2011), 98-111.

9   On this, see Andrew Davison, *The Love of Wisdom: An Introduction to Philosophy for Theologians* (London: SCM Press, 2013), 150.

10 This was an important theme for John Calvin, for instance. Examples include his *Commentary on Titus* (on Titus 1.12) and *Institutes of the Christian Religion* II.2.15.

11 *On the Literal Meaning of Genesis*, book 1, chapter 19, §39, translated by John Hammond Taylor (New York: Paulist Press, 1982), substituting 'non-believer' for 'infidel'.

12 The standard list of seven pivotal virtues in Christian thinking about human life is usually given as prudence (or practical wisdom), justice, moderation (or temperance), and courage (or fortitude), which are the natural (or cardinal) virtues, to which are added faith, hope, and love (or charity), from 1 Cor. 13.13, which are the supernatural (or theological) virtues. Central to the conviction of the authors of this book that the Church should value and support gay and lesbian sexual relationships is that we have seen, time and again, such relationships to be a nursery for these virtues.

13 That said, while the language of orientation may be new, the study of history shows that same-sex attraction and relationships certainly are not. There is a good deal of historical evidence of same-sex desire, sexual activity, and enduring romantic attachments between people of the same sex in the past. See, for instance, Laura Gowing, Michael Hunter and Miri Rubin (eds), *Love, Friendship and Faith in Europe, 1300 - 1800* (Basingstoke: Palgrave, 2005); Alan Bray, *The Friend* (Chicago: University of Chicago Press, 2003); Lillian Faderman, *Surpassing the Love of Men: Romantic Friendship and Love between Women from the Renaissance to the Present* (London: Women's Press, 1985).

14 To be frank, statements of that sort usually come down to one thing only, namely anal sex. That practice, however, is not unique to gay men. A major study by the US Department of Health and Human Services found that at least 30% of heterosexuals, aged 15-44, had engaged in anal sex at some point in their lives and around 40% of gay men, aged 15-44, had not. While there are differences by age, generation and culture, other studies in the USA and Europe show a similar pattern. See A. Chandra, US Department of Health and Human Services, *National Health Statistics Reports 36 (March 3, 2011): Sexual Behavior, Sexual Attraction, and Sexual Identity in the United States: Data From the 2006–2008 National Survey of Family. Growth* (www.cdc.gov/nchs/data/nhsr/nhsr036.pdf accessed 02/02/2016).

15 For a detailed discussion see Sophia M. Connell, *Aristotle on Female Animals: A Study of the Generation of Animals* (Cambridge University Press, 2016). As a concrete example of how our understanding of reproduction has moved on even rather recently, consider our appreciation of human ova. While we had known about ovaries since ancient times (Galen documents them, for instance), it wasn't until 1827 that Von Baer confirmed their role in reproduction, demonstrating to medical science that women have an active role in conception: that there is an ovum from the woman alongside the sperm from the man.

16 For instance, Thomas Aquinas, *Summa Contra Gentiles* III.122.9: 'after the sin of homicide whereby a human nature already in existence is destroyed, this type of sin appears to take next place, for by it the generation of human nature is precluded' (translation by Vernon J. Bourke, New York, NY: Hanover House, 1955).

17 For instance, Thomas Aquinas writing in *Summa Theologiae* II-II.154.12.

18 For example, see Evelyn E. Whitehead and James D. Whitehead, *A Sense of Sexuality* (New York: Doubleday, 1989).

19 Margaret A. Farley, *Just Love: A Framework for Christian Sexual Ethics* (London: Continuum, 2006), 215-232.

20 Research in psychology and psychiatry has shown that patterns of mental health among the non-heterosexual population do not relate to homosexuality as a 'mental disorder', but to the experience of stigma, prejudice and discrimination, which matches the experience of many other minority groups. See, for example, A. Chakraborty, S. McManus, T. S. Brugha, P. Bebbington and M. King, 'Mental health of the non-heterosexual population of England', *British Journal of Psychiatry*, 198.2 (2011), 143-8; Ilan Meyer, 'Prejudice, social stress, and mental health in lesbian, gay, and bisexual populations: Conceptual issues and research evidence', *Psychological Bulletin*, 129.5 (September 2003), 674–697.

21 Theologian, Susannah Cornwall has produced an excellent set of briefing papers, which are available at http://lincolntheologicalinstitute.com/iid-briefing-papers/.

22 See footnote 13 above.

23 The foundational work, based on data from 191 cultures, was undertaken by anthropologists Clennan Ford and Frank Beach. It was published in *Patterns of Sexual Behavior* (New York: Harper and Row, 1951), which they edited.

24 Gary J. Gates, (2011) 'How many people are lesbian, gay, bisexual and transgender?', The Williams Institute, UCLA, available as a pdf at http://williamsinstitute.law.ucla.edu/wp-content/uploads/Gates-How-Many-People-LGBT-Apr-2011.pdf. The third National Survey of Sexual Attitudes and Lifestyles (NATSAL 3, 2010-12) produced similar results with 1.5% of men self-defining their sexual identity as gay and 1.0 as bisexual, and 1.0% of women as lesbians and 1.4% as bisexual. For both sexes the proportion of some same-sex sexual contact was higher (8.0% and 11.5% respectively). See Catherine Mercer *et al.*, 'Changes in sexual attitudes and lifestyles in Britain through the life course and over time: Findings from the National Surveys of Sexual Attitudes and

Lifestyles (Natsal)' *The Lancet,* 382 No. 9907, 1781-1794, 30 November 2013, available at http://dx.doi.org/10.1016/S0140-6736(13)62035-8.

25 See Bruce Bagemihl, *Biological Exuberance: Animal Homosexuality and Natural Diversity* (New York: St Martin's Press, 1999). See also, Simon LeVay, *Gay, Straight, and the Reason Why: The Science of Sexual Orientation* (Oxford: Oxford University Press, 2011), 65-71. One clear example (well-known to farmers) concerns domesticated sheep. Around 10% of rams refuse to mate with females, but engage in sexual behaviour exclusively with other males, including anal penetration.

26 From a scientific perspective, the point is that there's a great deal more to study about human sexual attraction and activity than simply the gender of those involved. A parallel moral point is that gender hardly exhausts what matters in a relationship. On this see Andrew Davison, 'Gender: What difference does it really make' in *Church Times,* https://www.churchtimes.co.uk/articles/2014/4-april/comment/opinion/gender-what-difference-does-it-really-make.

27 See, for instance, Dale Goldhaber, *The Nature-Nurture Debates: Bridging the Gap* (Cambridge: Cambridge University Press, 2012); Michael Rutter, *Genes and behavior: Nature-Nurture Interplay Explained* (Malden: Wiley-Blackwell, 2006); Evelyn Fox Keller, *The Mirage of a Space between Nature and Nurture* (Durham: Duke University Press, 2010).

28 However, to say that the causes of each person's basic constitution are various – some genetic and some not – is not to say that each person chooses his or her constitution for his- or herself.

29 K. M. Kirk, J. M. Bailey, P. M. Dunne and N. G. Martin 'Measurement models for sexual orientation: A Community Twin Sample', *Behavioural Genetics* 30 (2000), 345-356. Available at https://genepi.qimr.edu.au/contents/p/staff/CV279.pdf.

30 Martin Johnson, 'A biological perspective on human sexuality', in B. Brooks-Gordon, L. Gelsthorpe, M. Johnson and A. Bainham (ed.), *Sexuality Repositioned: Diversity and the Law* (Oxford: Hart Publishing, 2004), 155-185, and especially 177.

31 A number of scientific studies have found differences in certain brain structures between heterosexual and homosexual men. The most significant of these relate to the discovery of a difference in the size of a particular region at the front of the hypothalamus (the third interstitial nucleus of the anterior hypothalamus), which is known to be involved in the regulation of male-typical sexual behaviours. In homosexual men this region appears to be smaller and more similar to that of women than to heterosexual men. Many scientists believe that prenatal hormones have a key role to play. So, for example, neuroscientist Simon LeVay concludes that 'it does seem to be reasonably well-established that prenatal androgen levels have a significant influence on sexual orientation in both men and women' (*Gay, Straight, and the Reason Why*, 156). Clearly more research needs to be undertaken, but there are strong indications that biological factors have an important role to play in the development of homosexual sexual attraction.

32 See Lord Sharkey's Pardon Bill in the House of Lords, and especially the Second Reading speeches by Lord Sharkey, Baroness Trumpington, and Lord Rees of Ludlow (Hansard 19 July 2009, Col. 1006-12).

33 See, for example: Pan American Health Organization/World Health Organization, '"Therapies" to change sexual orientation lack medical justification and threaten health', 17 May 2012. The statement is available at: http://www.paho.org/hq/index.php?option=com_content&view=article&id=6803&Itemid=1926. The strongest evidence for the success of conversion therapy came from a study by the eminent psychiatrist, Robert Spitzer, 'Can some gay men and lesbians change their sexual orientation? 200 Participants reporting a change from homosexual to

heterosexual orientation', *Archives of Sexual Behavior*, 32.5 (2003), 403–417. However in 2012, Spitzer admitted that his research was fatally flawed, adding 'I believe I owe the gay community an apology for my study making unproven claims of the efficacy of reparative therapy'. See https://exgaywatch. com/2012/04/spitzer-i-owe-the-gay-community-an-apology.

34 The president of Exodus International, Alan Chambers said that 'For quite some time we've been imprisoned in a worldview that's neither honoring toward our fellow human beings, nor biblical...From a Judeo-Christian perspective, gay, straight or otherwise, we're all prodigal sons and daughters. Exodus International is the prodigal's older brother, trying to impose its will on God's promises, and make judgments on who's worthy of His Kingdom. God is calling us to be the Father – to welcome everyone, to love unhindered.' See http://www. christianitytoday.com/gleanings/2013/june/alan-chambers- apologizes-to-gay-community-exodus.html.

35 On the question of choice, it is perhaps worth noting here that Christian understanding and discussion of people who are bisexual, who have the capacity for attraction to same-sex and other-sex partners, is often quite confused and confusing. In particular, it is sometimes assumed that bisexual people are inherently promiscuous. There is no clear evidence of this prejudice; indeed a recent study suggests that bisexual women, at least, are more likely to be monogamous than heterosexual women. See Lisa M. Diamond, 'Female bisexuality from adolescence to adulthood: Results from a 10-year longitudinal study', *Developmental Psychology* 44.1 (2008), 5-14.

36 Raising children is an increasingly prominent part of same-sex relationships, which has sometimes been the cause of concern or anxiety among Christians. Empirical investigations speak to this question. Research in developmental psychology has shown that heterosexual parents and same-sex parents do not differ in the quality of their parenting. Children raised by same-sex couples are as psychologically well-adjusted as

their heterosexual parent counterparts, and their gender development follows a typical trajectory. Indeed, a recent study of adopted children growing up in same-sex couple families found that the children in these families had lower levels of problems than for their heterosexual parent counterparts. Moreover, the gay fathers in this study showed lower levels of depression, and more positive parenting, than a heterosexual comparison group. However, the degree to which children in same-sex parent families are exposed to stigma remains a significant predictor of their outcomes. See S. Golombok, L. Mellish, S. Jennings, P. Casey, F. Tasker, and M. E. Lamb, 'Adoptive gay father families: Parent-child relationships and children's psychological adjustment', *Child Development* 85 (2014), 456–468. On the topic of same-sex parenting, see also Charlotte J. Patterson, 'Children of lesbian and gay parents: Psychology, law, and policy', *American Psychologist*, 64 (2009), 727-736; Judith Stacey and Timothy J. Biblarz, '(How) does the sexual orientation of parents matter?' *American Sociological Review*, 66 (2001), 159-183; F. Tasker and S. Golombok, *Growing up in a Lesbian Family* (New York: Guilford Press, 1997). We are grateful to Dr Sophie Zadeh for drawing our attention to this work.

37 When Paul appeals for the freedom of Onesimus in the Letter to Philemon, he does it on a personal basis, not by arguing that slavery itself is iniquitous.

38 Henry Ward Beecher, 'Peace be Still', in *Fast Day Sermons*, quoted by Mark Noll in *The Civil War as a Theological Crisis* (Chapel Hill, NC: University of North Carolina Press, 2006), 44. See the whole of this chapter by Noll, 'The Crisis over the Bible', for a closer examination of biblical defences of and attacks on slavery.

39 We are not suggesting that the work to combat slavery was completed when slavery and slave trading were made illegal. The abolition of contemporary slavery, in its many forms, is one of the most pressing social needs of our day. Pope Francis

and Justin Welby, the Archbishop of Canterbury, have been outspoken on that subject, not least in their support for the 'Global Freedom Network'. The website http://www.globalfreedomnetwork.org contains an archive of statements from both Anglican and Roman Catholic leaders on this topic.

40 Jack Rogers: *Jesus, the Bible & Homosexuality* (Louisville, KT: Westminster John Knox Press, 2009) – from a Reformed perspective; Daniel A. Helminiak, *What the Bible Really says about Homosexuality* (San Francisco: Alamo Square Press) – from a Roman Catholic perspective; John F. Dwyer: *Those 7 References: A Study of 7 References to Homosexuality in the Bible* (Booksurge, 2007) – Episcopal perspective; K. Renato Lings, *Love Lost in Translation: Homosexuality and the Bible* (Bloomington, IN: Trafford, 2013) – Evangelical Lutheran perspective; James W Brownson: *Bible, Gender, Sexuality: Reframing the Church's Debate on Same-Sex Relationships* (Grand Rapids, IN: Eerdmans, 2013) – evangelical perspective; Robert J. Gagnon *The Bible and Homosexual Practice: Texts and Hermeneutics* (Nashville : Abingdon Press, 2001) – conservative Reformed; Bernadette Brooten, *Love Between Women* (Chicago: Univeristy of Chicago Press, 1996) – from the perspective of ancient history.

41 Examples would include child birth (which made a woman unclean for seven days for a male child, and two weeks for a female child – Lev. 12.2-5), seminal discharges and menstruation (Lev. 15), eating hares or pigs (Lev. 11.6-7), or prawns (Lev. 11.10-12), sowing a field with two kinds of seed or wearing a garment made from two different materials (Lev. 19.19), and being tattooed (Lev. 19.28).

42 See Daniel Boyarin, 'Against Rabbinic Sexuality: Textual Reasoning and the Jewish Theology of Sex', in Gerard Loughlin (ed.), *Queer Theology* (Wiley-Blackwell, Oxford, 2007); K. Renato Lings, *Love Lost in Translation*, chapter 6; Jack Rogers, *Jesus the Bible and Homosexuality*, 68-69; Mary Douglas, *Purity and Danger: An Analysis of Concepts of Pollution and Taboo* (London, Routledge & Kegan Paul, 1966), 42-58.

43 See Dale B. Martin, *Sex and the Single Savior* (Louisville, KY: Westminster John Knox Press, 2006), especially chapter 3.

44 For detailed treatment of *malakoi* and *arsenokoites*, and their context and meaning, see K. Renato Lings, *Love Lost in Translation*, chapter 13.

45 John Chrysostom, *Homily I on Marriage*, quoted in Eugene Rogers (ed.), *Theology and Sexuality: Classic and Contemporary Readings* (Oxford: Blackwell, 2002), 90, from *Sermon on Marriage* in *On Marriage and Family Life*, trans. Catherine P. Roth and David Anderson (Crestwood, NY: St Vladimir's Seminary Press, 1997). Andrew Davison discusses the broader sense of 'offspring' as a good of marriage, for instance as Thomas Aquinas taught about it, in *Why Sacraments?*, 118-19.

46 See Augustine, *On the Good of Marriage*, 3.

47 To be strictly accurate, traditional Roman Catholic teaching does not require that *all* sexual acts must be open to the transmission of life. Infertile couples and those after child-bearing years are permitted to marry and have sexual intercourse in the Roman tradition (Canon 1084.3).

48 Rowan Williams, 'The Body's Grace' in Eugene F. Rogers, ed., *Theology and Sexuality: Classic and Contemporary Readings* (Oxford: Blackwell, 2002), 320.

49 What is stressed, indeed, is the similarly of Eve to Adam: 'This at last is bone of my bones and flesh of my flesh' (Gen. 2.23).

50 On this, see also Andrew Davison, 'Gender: What difference does it really make?'. This article questions what kind of argument is being made with claims about complementarity.

51 Or even Marconite.

52 In particular, Paul assumes here that everyone is intrinsically attracted to people of the opposite sex. Were that to be true, sex between two men or between two women *would* be going against their nature. (To this day, we would certainly not want a heterosexual person to go against his or her nature in that way.) With that assumption, Paul thought what other people thought at that time. Today, if we recognise that not all people *are*

constitutively attracted to people of the opposite sex, we need not blame Paul for thinking what he did. We would, however, be right to ask whether *Paul's own logic*, in this case, doesn't in fact suggest that gay and lesbian people in relationships today ought to act *according to their constitution*, which is as a gay or lesbian person, rather than against it.

53 Eugene Rogers, *Sexuality and the Christian Body*, see especially chapter 2; and Dale B. Martin, *Sex and the Single Savior*, see especially chapter 4.

54 *Surprised by Joy* (London: Geoffrey Bles, 1955), 196.

55 It is not beside the point of this book to note that these Montanists were regarded with considerable suspicion by Christian writers whose less antagonistic and dualist vision of the body and of human life came to be recognized as orthodoxy. Various forms of Gnosticism were criticised, for similar reasons.

56 Clement of Alexandria, *Paedogogus*. On Clement's attitudes to marriage and the 'encratites' ('self-controlled' ascetics), see Peter Brown, *The Body in Society: Men, Women and Sexual Renunciation in Early Christianity* (NY: Columbia University Press, 1988), chapter 6.

57 In his defence of marriage, *On the Good of Marriage*, Augustine wrote, nonetheless, that a marriage without sex was better than one with sex.

58 We see from Luther's 1520 'Appeal to His Imperial Majesty, and to the Christian Nobility of the German Nation, on the Reformation of Christianity' that he was aware that enforced clerical celibacy was not uniform in the Church – he appealed to 'the Greek Church'. He was also aware that compulsory celibacy was not the pattern in the early Church either, quoting 1 Tim. 3.2. It derives, to a great extent, from the reforming tradition of Gregory VII and the canonical revisions of Lateran II in 1139.

59 This has become 'modern tradition' for the Church of England, except in one specific case, where it has deviated from it. The

1991 House of Bishops document, *Issues in Human Sexuality*, holds gay and lesbian clergy to a different standard from gay and lesbian laypeople, by demanding celibacy of the clergy, but not from lay people; this policy remains in place today. This notion of compulsory celibacy without the *vocation* to celibacy is inherited from the periods of antiquity and the middle ages as we have seen. Those who call for gay and lesbian clergy to be able to marry, and thereby live in monogamous and permanent same-sex relationships, just as heterosexual clergy do, are in one sense asking the Church to come into line with what it said about priesthood, marriage, and the laity hundreds of years ago, as it has developed through the reading of Scripture and the experience of Christians such as Martin Luther and many others since his day.

60 Appendix in Randall Davidson (ed.), *The Six Lambeth Conferences 1867 – 1920* (London: SPCK, 1929), 44.

61 *The Lambeth Conference 1930: Encyclical Letter from the Bishops with the Resolutions and Reports* (London: SPCK, 1930) 44, 90, 91.

62 Nor, we might note, has it put an end to ecumenical agreement and cooperation.

63 Galen, *On the Usefulness of the Parts of the Body*, 14.5.

64 Thomas W. Laqueur, *Making Sex: Body and Gender from the Greeks to Freud* (Harvard University Press, 1990).

65 On the 'complementarty of the sexes', the rise of the middle class family, and evangelicalism, see Leonore Davidoff and Catherine Hall, *Family Fortunes: Men and Women of the English Middle Classes, 1789 - 1850* (London: Hutchinson, 1987).

66 Karl Barth, *Church Dogmatics* III/IV ed. G.W. Bromiley and T.F. Torrance (Edinburgh: T & T Clark, 1936 – 1975), 153.

67 Barth, *Church Dogmatics* III/IV, 154.

68 Another example is the Deceased Wife's Sister's Marriage Act of 1907.

69 Which is not to say that the ancient Hebrews were the only culture where that insight dawned.

70 *Institutes* I.13.1. The point had been made before Calvin. Bonaventure wrote that 'Christ the teacher, lowly as He was in the flesh, remained lofty in His divinity. It was fitting, therefore, that He and His teachings should be humble in word and profound in meaning: even as the Infant Christ was wrapped in swaddling clothes, so God's wisdom is wrapped in humble images' (Bonaventure, *Breviloquium*, trans. José de Vinck, Paterson, NJ: St Anthony Guild, 1963, prologue, 4.4).

71 For instance in Gal. 3.28, but we might think also of the examples of leadership occupied by women in the New Testament churches.

72 On why we bless things, people, and endeavours, and what that means, see Andrew Davison, *Blessing* (Canterbury Press, 2014). On blessing same-sex relationships, see especially 161-66.

73 This aspect of sexual relationships is stressed in our marriage liturgy.

74 *The Word and the World* (London: SCM Press, 1931), 108.

75 'Modern Theology and Biblical Criticism', an essay that Lewis read at Westcott House, Cambridge, on 11 May 1959. Published under that title in *Christian Reflections* (London: Geoffrey Bles, 1981), 152.

76 Thomas Schirmacher, 'Human Rights and Christian Faith', *Global Journal of Classic Theology*, 3.2 (2002).

77 Preface to the Declaration of Assent, Canon C15

78 One of us can tell the story of being at a large indie-rock concert a few years ago, in Columbus, Ohio. The place was full of under-forties; most were probably university students. It was the kind of occasion where hardly anyone, of a crowd of a couple of thousand, would have been anything other than a left-leaning liberal. As usual, there was a segment when the singer, Josh Ritter, stopped to talk to the crowd. All he talked about throughout that period was marriage, and every time he said the word 'marriage', the audience cheered. The more he talked about the value of marriage, in a world where we too easily

go astray, the louder the cheers; the closer he got – *we* might say – to a robust theological understanding of marriage, the more enthusiastic the cheering. That picture is the background to mission today, here as much as in the USA: young people, not just a conservative minority among them, are placing a new value on marriage, and they can't understand why we wouldn't want that for everyone (which is where the singer ended up too).

79 The Revd Dr Melanie Marshall, Chaplain of Lincoln College, Oxford.

80 The Revd Dr Megan Daffern, Chaplain, Jesus College, Oxford.

81 The Revd Richard Lloyd-Morgan, Dean of Divinity, Magdalen College, Oxford, and formerly Chaplain, King's College Cambridge.

82 The Revd Dr John Breadon, Assistant Chaplain at Eton College, director of the Wisdom Project, and formerly National Adviser for Further Education and Chaplaincy (Education Division), Archbishops' Council of the Church of England.

83 The Revd Dr Keith Riglin Chaplain, King's College, London.

84 Speech on his return from Australia and New Zealand, Westminster Central Hall, 30 January 1951, quoted in *Church Times*, 2 February 1951, 1.